University of Plymouth Library

Subject to status this item may be renewed
via your Voyager account

http://voyager.plymouth.ac.uk

Exeter tel: (01392) 475049
Exmouth tel: (01395) 255331
Plymouth tel: (01752) 232323

THE COSTS OF THE COMMON
AGRICULTURAL POLICY

The Costs of the Common Agricultural Policy

Allan E. Buckwell, David R. Harvey,
Kenneth J. Thomson and Kevin A. Parton

CROOM HELM
London & Canberra

© 1982 A.E. Buckwell, D.R. Harvey, K.J. Thomson and K.A. Parton
Croom Helm Ltd, 2-10 St John's Road, London SW11

British Library Cataloguing in Publication Data

The Costs of the common agricultural policy.
    1. Agriculture — European Community countries —
    Economic aspects 2. Common Agricultural Policy
    I. Buckwell, Allan E.
    338.1'81   HD1920.5
    ISBN 0-7099-0671-4

Printed and bound in Great Britain by
Biddles Ltd, Guildford and King's Lynn

CONTENTS

TABLES AND FIGURES

Tables

Figures

ACKNOWLEDGEMENTS

The authors are grateful to the Social Science
Research Council, whose research grant, at a time
of severe financial difficulties, enabled us to
carry out the work reported in this study. We are
also indebted to our colleagues, especially
Professor Christopher Ritson and Mr. Lionel Hubbard,
within and outside the Department of Agricultural
Economics at the University of Newcastle-upon-Tyne,
for their contributions, conscious or unconscious,
to the processes of argument and counter-argument
which characterised this piece of research.

Chapter 1

AGRICULTURE : THE PILLAR AND THE PROBLEM OF CAP

EUROPEAN INTEGRATION

During the first fifteen years of the European
Community, which came into operation on January 1st
1958, enormous progress was made in building up in-
stitutions and organisations to implement the pro-
visions of the Treaty of Rome. Whilst the Treaty
contained articles for common policies in many
areas, including agriculture, customs duties, competition, social provision and transport, it became
apparent that progress towards other economic
common economic policies would be difficult without
agreement on a Common Agricultural Policy (CAP)
which would level food costs in member countries and
eliminate trade barriers on agricultural produce.
As the six founder members gradually harmonised
their own systems of agricultural support, they
transferred the financial responsibilities for the
agricultural policy from their own exchequers to the
Community budget. Thus by the time that the CAP was
in full operation in 1969 agricultural support
accounted for most of the budget. That it was
possible to create a common agricultural policy at
all out of the disparate levels and methods of agricultural support was a testament to the ingenuity
and common political will of the member states. It
was thus no exaggeration to refer to the CAP as a
pillar of the Community.
     However, during the 1970s the founding fathers'
vision of the gradual integration of economic and
social policies within the Community, and a corresponding convergence of economic activity in the
member states, suffered a series of setbacks. No
sooner had the original six members achieved common
agricultural prices at the end of the sixties, than
currency movements, following the collapse of the
Bretton Woods fixed exchange rate regime, caused

1

national agricultural price levels to diverge.
Shortly after these upheavals came the 1973 oil
crisis. This, and the subsequent rounds of energy
problems, provided a challenge to the Community to
devise a common energy policy. However, the disparate circumstances and interests of the member states
have outweighed the perceived benefits of a common
approach. To compound these difficulties for
further integration of the Community, the enlargement in 1973 from six to nine members, and the pros-
pective enlargement in the 1980s to twelve members,
have presented both a greater need for economic convergence and at the same time many more obstacles to
achieving it. Whilst the Community has been
struggling to cope with the changed financial,
energy and political circumstances, the world
economy generally has moved into recession.
    This is the backdrop against which the
Community's economic and financial difficulties of
unemployment and inflation are present in all member
states but to differing degrees, and governments
have rather different ideas about priorities and
methods to attack these problems. The result is
that, despite the attempt to forge greater monetary
union through the European Monetary System, the real
economies of the Community show few signs of convergence. In fact governments not only show little
enthusiasm for relinquishing sovereignty over economic and social policies but are being subjected to
great pressures to move in the opposite direction
towards nationalistic appraisal of Community policies and even towards protectionism.

THE AGRICULTURAL AND BUDGETARY PROBLEMS

There are two elements in the current financial
problems in the Community; the rapid growth of the
budget towards the ceiling of funds which can be
raised under the existing legislation, and the
alleged inequitable distribution of the burden of
the budget. Since 1970 the total EC budget has
grown at about 22 per cent per annum, although the
current total of 16 billion (thousand million)
European Units of Account (EUA) is still less than
one per cent of Community GNP. If the budget continues to grow apace and if growth in Community GNP
slows or even stops then the budget will soon assume
a significant portion of total economic activity.
Within the overall budget, the share of the European
Agricultural Guidance and Guarantee Fund (known generally by its French acronym FEOGA) is currently
about 75 per cent. This share has varied from year

to year but has never been less than 70 per cent.
The growth of the budget is almost entirely a consequence of the growth in the costs of agricultural
support.

A thorough study to apportion the increase in
agricultural support costs amongst its contributory
causes has not been carried out, but a few general
points can be made. First, the volume of agricultural output has grown rapidly, primarily as a
result of technical improvements in crop and animal
yields rather than increases in the areas of land
utilised or livestock numbers. In turn, yields per
animal and per hectare have increased because of the
adoption of improved varieties and breeds, the increased mechanisation of agriculture and the greater
use of purchased inputs. This technical progress
has not been a purely self-motivated phenomenon from
within the farming sector but to a large extent has
been stimulated by the Common Agricultural Policy
itself. When society indicates that it wishes to
transfer income to the farming sector through a
continuing and open-ended system of price supports
for the output of the sector, it is no surprise that
the industry and the associated businesses up and
down-stream should try to take the maximum advantages of such largesse by investment in fixed capital, research and development so as to increase
output. The important point is not so much that
real agricultural prices have actually risen, rather
that farmers have been led to expect that their
costs can be recouped and their incomes preserved
regardless of the volume of output they jointly produce. Whilst the pace of technological advance undoubtedly has been stimulated by the price support
system of the CAP, this is not the only factor.
Member countries have their own nationally financed
investment aids which have further contributed to
this trend. Two of the stated objectives of the CAP
in the Treaty of Rome were concerned with improving
agricultural productivity[1] and providing stability
in the market. That these have been achieved is
beyond doubt. The costs of achieving them, however,
have been rather high.

The issue of whether the burden of the Community budget has been inequitably distributed amongst
the member countries was the centre of considerable
argument during 1979 and 1980. From the point of
view of understanding the real causes of the problem
and moving towards a real cure, it is unfortunate
that the debate has often been conducted as simply a
budgetary problem, and at times, as a purely British
budgetary problem. It was known at the time of

3

United Kingdom entry in 1973 that an agricultural
support policy based on subsidising exports, storing
surplus production and taxing imports was likely to
result in little direct budgetary expenditure in the
United Kingdom, which is a net importer of most temperate zone agricultural produce. This is precisely
what has happened, although the effect of the
commodity price boom of 1972-74 did delay its onset
until the last few years of the 1970s. What was not
generally expected at the time of entry was that the
offsets to the budgetary cost to Britain of the CAP
would not materialise. Whilst this is not the place
to discuss the success or failure of U.K. balance of
trade in manufactures with the EC, it is reasonable
to point out that it was not generally predicted
that the agricultural fund would grow at such a pace
that it would swamp the development of other funds
in the Community budget, nor that a severe recession
would dampen the urge and reduce the ability to pay
for further common economic and social policies.

ASSESSING THE COST OF AGRICULTURAL POLICY

It is important to realise that any common Community
policies will, and indeed should, involve inter-
country transfers. Within a single country, if it
is judged that the free operation of the market in
any sector of the economy does not result in the
desired level of output, incomes or prices, then
policies are often introduced to steer the sector to
the required position. Such policies will inevitably involve transfers between different groups
within the country, usually from some group outside
the sector to a group inside the sector. When the
policy is supra-national, then unless the protected
sector of each country is of similar size and
suffers disadvantages to a similar degree, there
will result inter-country transfers. If such transfers did not occur then there might be little point
in the common supra-national policy. In the case of
agriculture, with wide divergences between the relative size and structure of the sector in each member
state, it is inevitable that inter-country transfers
will arise from any common agricultural policy. The
important point is therefore whether the transfers
are having the desired effects and whether they are
being effected in the most efficient manner. In
more concrete terms, the relevant question is not to
do with whether one member country is paying a disproportionate amount of the agricultural support
cost, but whether the method of support used is the
most effective way of transferring income to the

4

target groups.

It is most important to realise that there is not just one measure of the cost of the common agricultural policy. The political debate of the last two years has focussed almost entirely on the net budgetary costs to particular member states. This ignores the cost to consumers throughout the Community who pay more for their food than they might do under a different policy. It also ignores the cost of the misallocation of resources resulting from the overexpansion of agricultural output. The elaborate exercise in market regulations represented by the CAP sets up enormous transfers between groups (consumers, taxpayers and producers) within each member state and between the member states. In order to agree the most desirable direction for change in the CAP it is necessary to consider all of these transfers and not just a small subset of them.

Whichever measures of cost are considered to be relevant, it should be realised that the magnitude of the cost measured depends on the alternative policy specified. This is a fundamental point and yet it has received virtually no attention throughout the fierce debate on the costs to Britain of participation in the CAP.

It is a basic proposition in economics that the cost of any activity can only meaningfully be measured in relation to some alternative activity. If there really is no alternative then in one sense there is no <u>cost</u> from continuing the status quo. In the context of the CAP this means that if it is desired to measure the balance of payments cost to Britain of the current arrangements for agricultural commodities, then this can only be calculated with reference to some specified alternative set of arrangements. Too often this kind of calculation is done by comparing the situation with the policy to that without any policy at all - that is, under a completely unrestrained market. In doing so it is not often spelt out that this is the comparison being made; neither is it argued that the free market is the most preferred state.

The belief underlying the present study is that both the growth of the Community budget and the distribution of the benefits and burden arising from the budget are inextricably linked to the Common Agricultural Policy. Solutions to these problems, if they exist at all, will not be found in changes in the budgetary mechanism but only in changes in the CAP itself. The danger of ignoring this point is that temporary modifications to the budgetary

5

mechanism (as were made arising out of the summit conference in Dublin in 1975 and by the Council of Ministers in Brussels in May 1980) only complicate the negotiating position of member states and delay attention being given to the underlying problem, allowing it to grow in magnitude and complexity.

The defenders of the CAP often claim that, as it is the most significant agreed common policy, it represents a vital pillar in the whole Community structure. If true, this does not augur well for the future of the Community because the pillar contains some deep cracks and flaws. Descriptions of these flaws abound and there are also many published discussions of general alternatives to the present CAP.[2] However, apart from the rather narrow studies of the balance of payments costs to Britain of the current CAP compared to no Common agricultural policy at all*, there are few systematic studies of the nature and size of transfer payments between consumers, producers, taxpayers and nations of a range of alternative changes to the CAP.

This study is intended as a step in that direction. The next two chapters respectively review the development of the CAP and its current plight, and set out an analytical framework for examining the impact of changes to CAP. Chapter 4 discusses the literature to date on assessments of the costs of CAP showing how there are a great many alternative estimates of even a relatively narrow definition of the cost. Chapters 5 to 8 present, an outline of the method used in this study, discussion of four alternative policies used in the analysis, and results by commodity groups and by country. Chapter 9 considers in more detail the distributional impacts of policy changes and also compares the efficiency of policies in achieving particular objectives. Chapter 10 summarises the main findings of this study.

NOTES

1.   In this context improving agricultural product-ivity is interpreted as increasing the volume of agricultural output.
2.   See for example: (A) Professors Uri Koester and Stefan Tangerman, 'Supplementing Farm Price Policy by Direct Income Payments', European Review of Agricultural Economics, 4 (1), 1977, pp. 7-31. German economists who discuss direct income support.   (B) Professor John S. Marsh,

---

*   These studies are reviewed in Chapter 4.

UK Agricultural Policy within the European Community, Centre for Agricultural Strategy, Reading, 1978, who favours abandoning common prices except for trade purposes; the suggestion by: (C) E. Pisani, 'European Socialists Demand CAP Reform', Agra-Europe Weekly, Vol. 869 (1980), El-E2, for a scheme of digressive pricing beyond a given level of output; and (D) the Commission of the European Communities, Reflections on the Common Agricultural Policy, COM (80) 800, Brussels, 1980, which favours a general extension of producer co-responsibility as a way of improving the budget position.

Chapter 2

THE COMMON AGRICULTURAL POLICY

There are numerous reviews[1] of the Common Agricultural Policy (CAP), and it is not the purpose in the present chapter to provide a comprehensive treatment. Rather, the discussion will concentrate on specific details relevant to the remainder of this study. The chapter commences with a description of the development of the CAP, its objectives, and the instruments which are applied in the pursuit of these objectives. The method of financing the CAP is examined to show how the budgetary transfers of the policy arise. The final part of the chapter describes a projection from the current situation to identify the likely future pressures on the CAP.

THE DEVELOPMENT OF THE CAP TO 1970

The process of post-war European integration is based on a number of international agreements commencing with the Treaty of Paris in 1951. This treaty involved only the coal and steel industries, but reflected a general desire in the countries concerned for greater co-operation in economic, social and political issues.

The Treaty of Rome established the European Economic Community in 1957. For the six signatories - West Germany, France, Italy, the Netherlands, Belgium and Luxembourg - the first significant step was to establish a common market by the removal of barriers on intra-Community trade. For industrial products, internal tariffs were dismantled and internal tariff-free trade with a common customs tariff was achieved by 1968. This progress was assisted by the initial low level of trade barriers in such products, the general favourable climate for economic growth in the countries involved, and the wider multinational tariff cutting exercises under the General Agreement on Tariffs and Trade (GATT).

9

In agriculture, the position was somewhat
different. The founder members of the Community
each had a complex set of agricultural policies so
the Treaty of Rome was able to outline a common plan
for agriculture only in broad terms. This involved
an exploratory negotiation stage of up to three
years, followed by a gradual alignment of policies
by 1970. The five objectives of the agricultural
policy in the Treaty of Rome[2] are:

(i)   To increase agricultural produc-
      tivity by developing technical
      progress and by ensuring the ra-
      tional development of agricultural
      production and the optimum utilis-
      ation of the factors of production,
      particularly labour.

(ii) To ensure thereby a fair standard
      of living for the agricultural
      population, particularly by the
      increasing of the individual
      earnings of persons engaged in
      agriculture.

(iii) To stabilize agricultural markets.

(iv) To guarantee regular supplies of
      food to consumers.

(v)   To ensure reasonable prices in
      supplies to consumers.

The first part of the negotiation stage was the
Stresa Conference in 1958 at which were established
further subsidiary objectives for example, the en-
couragement of family farming, and the preservation
of rural areas through rural industrialisation.
It became the task of the Commission of the EEC
to devise policies which would promote these objectives. The introduction of the CAP required agreement on the type of instrument and the level of
support. The policy which evolved encompasses three
principles viz. free trade within the Community,
Community preference in trade, and common financial
responsibilities. By the end of 1960 the Council of
Ministers had accepted a system of market support
consistent with the principles. Within this basic
framework it was necessary to settle the detailed,
often commodity-specific, interests of the individual countries. Not surprisingly, there was some
hard bargaining between the member states before the
details of applying the common policy were agreed
for cereals, pigmeat, poultry, eggs, fruit and

vegetables and wine early in 1962, and for beef and veal, dairy products and vegetable oils late in 1963.

The intention was gradually to harmonise the different price levels in each country during a transition period. In addition, a mechanism for financing Community policies on a common basis between the Six was to be determined. This evolution of the CAP has been described in detail.[3] Suffice to say here that after a number of crises, including the withdrawal of the French delegates from the Council of Ministers for six months, the transition to a common price policy was completed in 1970. The method of financing, however, has remained in a state of flux during the 1970s.

The outcome was an agricultural policy which was more protectionist than the national policies that it replaced. The principal reasons were that (i) countries with high levels of price support wanted high common prices, (ii) the range of products covered by the policy was expanded because each country had special interests in particular commodities (e.g. tobacco in Italy), and (iii) there was less pressure on individual countries to limit price increases because of common financing.[4]

The legal expression of the CAP consists of regulations, directives and decisions. Regulations override national laws and apply throughout the Community. Directives are expressions of objectives to which all members are committed but which they can implement as they wish. Decisions are binding commitments on named governments, organisations or individuals.

At a higher level of control, changes in policy can only be made by the Council of Ministers. The procedure for such changes is that the Commission is invited to propose changes, or it may do so spontaneously. These proposals emerge after a process of consultation and lobbying at the European level with the European Economic and Social Committee and various trade and consumer organisations. These organisations in turn consult with corresponding interests in the member states. Commission proposals are finally agreed, amended or rejected by the Council of Ministers. These procedures apply both to the occasional changes or innovations in agricultural policy and also to the annual agricultural price-fixing process each spring.

The implementation of the regulations and directives which make up the CAP is the responsibility of the Commission. The detailed administration is conducted partly by the Commission and partly in each member state by intervention

11

agencies. The weekly operation of the support
system is monitored and discussed by commodity man-
agement committees comprising officials from the
Commission and each member state.

MARKET SUPPORT

The principal instruments with which the CAP
supports market prices are variable import levies
and export refunds on trade with third countries,
and intervention buying on domestic markets by
government agencies. This apparatus is seen most
clearly in use in the cereals and dairy produce
sectors and is supplemented or partly replaced in
these and other sectors by a host of other instruments of support. These include: producer subsidies, for example for rice, olive oil and durum
wheat; payments called slaughter premiums for beef;
consumer and processor subsidies for butter and skim
milk powder respectively; production quotas for
sugar and import quotas for some live animals and
certain vegetables; and aids for private storage for
cereals, wine, flax and hemp. These regulations
cover 73 per cent of Community final agricultural
output. To this may be added poultry produce,
quality wine and fruit and vegetables for which
there exist regulations but not common prices and
this brings the proportion of output covered by the
CAP to over 90 per cent. With the agreement on a
sheepmeat regime in 1980, the only significant
commodity not covered by CAP regulations is
potatoes.
     The degree of support offered by the CAP is
not uniform across all commodities. This is illustrated by Table 2.1 in which EC import prices are
expressed as a percentage of the third country
offer price. This is an extremely crude measure of
the degree of protection because the numerator is
not exactly correlated with producer prices in the
EC and the denominator is not the price at which
substantial imports could be purchased. Nonetheless
the figures are some indication that (a) the overall
degree of nominal price support offered by CAP is
one point three to three times the world price, and
(b) the protection is highest for dairy produce,
next highest for olive oil and maize, at an intermediate level for other cereals and lowest for pigmeat and sugar. Not shown in the table is that
these indicators tended to increase from 1973/74 to
about 1977 and have since declined a little although
there are deviations around this pattern.

Table 2.1: Relative Price Support by Commodity
            in the EC 1979/80

Commodity	EC entry price as a percentage of Third-Country offer price
	%
Butter	411
Skim Milk Powder	379
Olive Oil	193
Maize	190
Oil Seeds	185
Common Wheat	163
Barley	161
Durum Wheat	159
Pigmeat	152
White Sugar	131

Source: EC Commission, Agricultural
         Situation in the Community, 1980
         Report.

    The floor of the market is the intervention
price, at which the intervention authorities of the
Community are obliged to purchase any eligible production which is offered to them. To protect the
market from lower priced imports from non-member
states a threshold, or minimum import, price is
fixed at a level above intervention price. An
import tax, or variable levy, is imposed to raise
the price of such imports to Community levels.
Because the world price varies, this import tax must
vary correspondingly to ensure a stable internal
price level. Conversely, when agricultural commodities are exported from the Community, an export subsidy or refund is paid to the exporter so that competition on the generally lower priced world markets
is possible.

GREEN MONEY

The intention in the original CAP design was to have
a uniform set of threshold and intervention prices
throughout the Community for a particular product.
To achieve this, the target, intervention and
threshold prices were all agreed in terms of

European units of account, EUA,* which were then
translated into member state currencies using the
fixed parities between these currencies and the unit
of account. By 1969 initial differences between
prices in member states had been eliminated and
common prices, as intended, were in force across the
Community. This situation was soon disturbed, however, by the instability on world currency markets.
As the value of the currency of one member changes
in relation to others, and in particular to the EUA,
so its internal agricultural support price changes.
Generally this is deemed undesirable in the countries concerned so members are permitted to use
rates of exchange between their currency and the EUA
different to the market rates. The artificial rates
of exchange used are called the representative rates
or more commonly green rates. Their effect is that
support prices are differentiated between members and
to prevent this in itself from further distorting
trade a system of border taxes and subsidies called
Monetary Compensatory Amounts (MCAs) is used.
Initially the system of green rates and MCAs was
considered a temporary measure to enable each country to maintain relatively stable support prices
when measured in its own currency. However despite
the efforts to restore stability in European exchange rates through the European joint float and
latterly the European Monetary System, differentiated prices and MCAs have become a continuing feature of the CAP.

A member country with an appreciating currency
and hence, in the absence of the MCA corrective
mechanism, falling import prices has an MCA tax on
its imports from other Community members, and for
its extra-EC imports the variable levy is increased
by the amount of the MCA. The country's exports to
other member states is no longer at the common EC
price, but at the common price less an MCA subsidy.
Refunds on exports to the rest of the world similarly are increased by the MCA subsidy. The effects
of the MCA system on countries with depreciating
currencies are the opposite of this.

The expenditures which arise from the operation
of the intervention and export refund systems including MCAs as well as the outlays on other production and consumption subsidies are paid from the

---

* The denomination of the unit of account used
for this purpose has changed several times, the
interested reader is referred to Fearn and Irving
for details.[5]

14

guarantee section of the Agricultural Guidance and
Guarantee Fund of the Community. Agricultural
levies, less ten per cent retained for administration, are an important source of funds for the
Community budget.

STRUCTURAL POLICY

In addition to the price support measures described
above, the Community also operates a system of
structural improvement measures. There are some
twenty identifiable situations where structural
assistance has been provided by the EC, ranging from
land drainage to vocational training, and from
eradication of cattle diseases to providing aid for
fisheries producer groups. More than half of the
expenditure has been on farm modernisation measures,
schemes to encourage farmers to give up dairy cows
and the provision of infrastructure in disadvantaged
areas.
      Expenditure on structural measures is financed
from the guidance section of FEOGA. However the
amount of money spent in this way has been extremely
limited. It was originally envisaged that it would
amount to one third of guarantee section expenditure, but this level has not been approached. The
Commission has continually sought ways to direct
more Community resources, through guidance section
schemes, towards the relatively disadvantaged sectors of the agricultural industry.

FINANCING THE CAP

The present system of financing the Community budget
as a whole comprises three elements: agricultural
levies arising from variable levies on imported
agricultural produce and production levies on sugar
and milk; duties raised on imported manufactures
through the common customs tariff (CCT); and a
contribution from value added tax (VAT) collected
on consumer expenditure in member countries. These
three components are known as the Community's 'own
resources'. The full own resource system has only
been in operation since 1979, and its evolution has
been exceedingly tortuous, but the details are not
relevant to this tract. The important point is
that, prior to the system of own resources, the
total funds raised each year was the amount required
to cover obligatory spending under the market
support regulations of CAP plus whatever other expenditure the Council agreed to. In contrast, the

own resource system contains a ceiling on the amount which can be raised, because of the rules concerning the VAT based contribution.

The total amount to be raised through VAT is determined each year by the Commission as the amount required to balance the budget after income from levies and CCT has been set against total expenditure. The contributions from each member is expressed as a percentage of a harmonised VAT base (for example 0.75% in 1979). In this way countries contribute in proportion, broadly speaking, to their level of total expenditure on goods and services on which VAT is charged. Because growth in Community expenditure, over 70 per cent of which is agricultural expenditure, has considerable exceeded the growth in levies and duties, the proportion of VAT required rose in 1980 and is projected to rise again in 1981. The scope for this to continue is limited because the Community has legislated an upper bound to this VAT contribution of one per cent.

The yield of a given percentage point of VAT and of the CCT expand through real economic growth in member states and, of course, through general price inflation. The revenues raised through agricultural import and production levies are partly affected by Community price decisions, but there is a large unpredictable element in the yield from import levies because of world price variation.

Figure 2.1 shows the collective effect of these factors. The annual growth from 1978 to 1981 of the maximum funds which could be raised through own resources has been about 11 per cent. This is projected forwards at 10 per cent per annum. The average rate of growth in FEOGA guarantee expenditure 1973-81 has been about 18 per cent but it has varied considerably. In fact in 1973/74 it fell due to high world prices and the first enlargement of the Community, which stimulated trade diversion and enabled some saving on export refunds on trade, for example, with the United Kingdom.

Since 1978, there has been a slackening in the rate of growth of expenditure. The average growth rate from 1974 to 1978 was nearly 27 per cent. Since then it has almost halved, to 14 per cent, in 1979 and 1980, mirroring the changes in FEOGA guarantee expenditure. The explanatory factors in 1981 were the desire to expand non-agricultural spending, and the need to finance special payments to some member states, notably the U.K. Whether the budget ceiling is reached in 1982, 1983 or not at all depends on the assumptions made about agricultural

**FIGURE 2.1   THE COMMUNITY BUDGET AND AGRICULTURAL
EXPENDITURES**

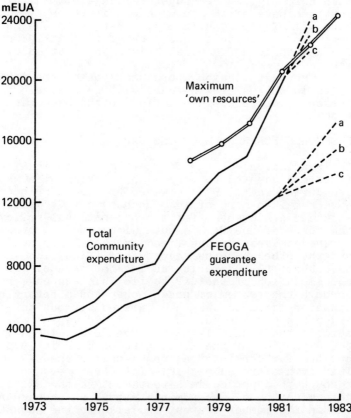

a, b, c   Incorporate alternative Commission projections of expenditure

Source: Commission of the European Communities:
     (i)   Preliminary Draft Budget 1981 Vol. 7/8
           Section III Com (80) 250.

     (ii) Budget appropriations, Official Journal of the
           European Communities, various.

support expenditure and on non-agricultural spending. If the growth in the former falls to the
Commission's target of half the rate of growth of
own resources, that is about 5½ per cent per annum,
then not only is the budget ceiling left inviolate
but the share of the total expenditure on agriculture will fall. Conversely, a return to the growth
rates in agricultural spending of the mid-1970s
could lead to a financial crisis in a matter of
months.

The next section appraises some of the developments in the CAP in the early 1980s and the
pressures it faces in addition to the budgetary
problems.

PRESSURES FOR REFORM OF THE CAP

The regulations of the CAP have been continually refined and adapted to cope with changing circumstances during the 1970s. However the broad principles
have remained more or less unchanged. It is a remarkable achievement for a supra-national policy of
the scope of the CAP to have withstood the pressures
of the collapse of the fixed exchange rate regime
and the other external economic difficulties which
have beset the Community during the decade. The
accommodation of the CAP to flexible exchange rates
through the system of green money and monetary compensatory amounts was not achieved without considerable strains but the system did manage to give
members the flexibility they required. In addition
the expansion of the EC to nine members in 1973
created further internal problems for the CAP.
That it has proved possible for CAP to evolve
through this period is a testament to the skill and
determination of its administrators at the centre
and in the member states, and also to the robust-
ness of the policy instruments. However the difficulties of the 1970s have left their mark and the
important question now is whether the CAP can with-
stand the present difficulties and the problems in
prospect.

The most widely criticised aspect of the CAP is
the production of surpluses. The problem has been
most obvious in the case of dairy products, but
cereals, sugar, beef, wine and olive oil are other
commodities that have given cause for concern. The
surplus problems have arisen because policies which
seemed reasonable when the CAP commenced operation
have continued despite increases in the degree of
self-supply. Initially prices were set to achieve a

18

farm income objective. At the time this created little problem of contradictions with other policy goals, but continued emphasis on maintaining farm incomes through price policy has induced over-production, curtailed growth in consumption and resulted in costly surpluses.

The initial reaction to the appearance of chronic surpluses over and above subsidised exports has been to develop measures to dispose of them rather than to change the signals which gave rise to them in the first place. Thus a plethora of measures to encourage domestic utilisation of surpluses has been devised. For example in the early days a 'denaturing premium' was paid on milling wheat which was used for livestock feed. Political opposition to this blatant destruction of food stopped the scheme in 1974 since when the Community has tried to be more subtle in its disposal methods. The current principal method of internal disposal is to subsidise consumption. This is done in such a way as to minimise the effect on commercial purchases, for example in the milk sector by subsidising feed compounders to use milk powder, by providing consumer butter subsidies to those in receipt of social assistance payments, and by subsidising school milk. Such measures have been expensive and, whilst keeping stocks to manageable levels, have done nothing to stem the over-production.

Some attempts to deal directly with the problem of over-supply at source have been made, for example, through the introduction of production quotas for sugar in 1975, and through a variety of measures in the milk sector which started in 1969. These include incentive payments, to encourage cessation of marketing of milk, to slaughter cows, and to convert dairy herds to beef herds. The impact of such measures has not been great. In the case of dairying the total herd size in the Community has not been noticeably affected and production has continued to rise. Another line of attack on milk output has been made more recently through the introduction of co-responsibility levies in 1977. These are taxes collected from dairies on milk deliveries. However the size of the levy has been small and, given the exemption for small producers in less favoured areas,[6] it has neither discouraged growth in production to any great extent nor has it collected much revenue.

A more significant attack on the remorseless growth in agricultural output has been the cut in common prices in real terms in 1979/80 and 1980/81.

For these two years nominal price increases of about two per cent per annum coupled with considerably greater rates of price inflation in some countries has resulted in a substantial fall in real prices, and in turn in real farm incomes.* The supply effects of this have not fully shown through because of the lags in production. However farm incomes have fallen significantly, although not uniformly, across the Community, and this constitutes a further pressure for change.

Another problem of the present method of price support is its inequity. It must be accepted that any Community policy involves transfers between individuals, sectors of the European economy and between member states. However, the CAP is financed by taxpayers, through governmental transfers to the Community, and by consumers, through relatively high food prices. The target beneficiaries of the policy are farmers. There is a prima facie case that the transfers effected through high food prices are regressive. Cross-country, and within-country, evidence shows that there is a negative relationship between the proportion of expenditure on food and income levels. Thus the poor bear a disproportionate share of the burden of this transfer. At the receiving end, it is clear that the CAP has not been of particular benefit to low income farmers. Because producers benefit from price support in proportion to their output, a large part of the support accrues to the largest and most well-off section of the industry. Even here much of the benefit is capitalised into land values, which does not always benefit the farm operator.

Transfers between member states as a result of the CAP occur because of the particular structure of the economies of the members. For example the United Kingdom makes a large net budgetary contribution because, as a food deficit country, it receives a relatively low level of CAP expenditure as an offset to the budget contributions made. In addition, there is a food-cost transfer from consumers to producers which arises because of the high price of food under the CAP. This also entails transfers from the United Kingdom to other member countries because, as a food importer, some of the beneficiaries of such a food-cost transfer are producers in other member states. The inequity of these inter-country

---

* Note that because of adjustments to green rates some member states have been able to engineer price rises in these years despite the overall downward turn in common prices.[7]

transfers, particularly these affecting the United Kingdom, was the source of considerable political discussion in 1980 and dominated the April summit of EC leaders in Luxembourg and also the discussions of the Council of Ministers in May of that year. However, the discussions concentrated on budgetary corrections rather than the causes of these undesirable transfer effects.

Another source of difficulty for the CAP has been its trade effects on third countries. The high level of protection restricts the quantity of overseas food products sold in the Community. Moreover, subsidised Community exports tend to undercut other exporters in the third country markets. Not only has CAP affected the volume of trade for third countries, but it has increased the volatility of the world market by insulating the Community from the effects of internal and external production and consumption fluctuations.[8] An indirect repercussion is that pressure has been placed on the EC in trade negotiations such as the Tokyo Round of GATT. Attempts were made by various countries during these talks to bring about a liberalisation of world trade in agricultural commodities. The CAP became a fundamental obstacle to this objective. The EC, as the largest importer of agricultural products, would not negotiate (or could not because of the problem of achieving a nine-member agreed position) on its agricultural policy. Little progress was therefore made in gaining for agricultural trade the degree of liberalisation achieved for other products.

A further sensitive issue connected with third country trade has been the dissatisfaction felt within the Community about exporting commodities, such as butter, at highly subsidised prices to countries in Eastern Europe. The consequences of this policy is that consumers in Eastern Europe receive certain EC milk products at prices far below those paid by consumers in the Community, at a time when East-West relationships have become particularly sensitive.

A final significant matter which is expected to cause substantial pressure on the CAP is the further enlargement of the EC planned to occur during the 1980s. Though space prohibits a comprehensive treatment of the issue here, a few salient points can be made.[9] The impact on the CAP of this second enlargement will probably be much greater than when the United Kingdom, Denmark and Ireland joined in 1973. The entry of Greece, already achieved in January 1981, and, later, Portugal and Spain will increase the GDP of the Community by about one tenth, its population by one fifth, agricultural output by about one quarter, and people engaged in agriculture by about one half. Hence, it can be expected that agriculture will be a central theme in the negotiations on accession, with efforts to raise agricultural productivity being of specific importance.

Increased importance of Mediterranean agricultural products, which enlargement implies, is also likely to cause difficulties. Higher Community price levels may induce expanded output of these products in the applicant countries, which will compete directly with production in Italy and Southern France. Also, there is an array of problems that entry of three new countries will bring concerning relations in agricultural trade with third countries. For example, the entry of Greece will ensure more favourable treatment of its exports to the rest of the Community than those of Turkey, a country with Association Agreements with the EC. Some sort of compensatory measure may be necessary for Turkey. A third type of difficulty relates to the changing consumption patterns away from Mediterranean products, with rising incomes in the applicant countries. This may necessitate shifts in production in these countries, for example, towards more livestock products.

CONCLUSION

The CAP has been the main expression of post war moves towards economic integration in Europe. It has showed a remarkable ability to adapt and survive in the face of considerable external strains, particularly exchange rate fluctuations. However, pressures on the policy itself have been increasing over the last few years, particularly with respect to problems of surplus production and its excessive budgetary expenditure, inequitable treatment of groups of individuals and member countries, trade effects on third countries, and enlargement of the Community. Whether the CAP can continue to be adjusted to accommodate these pressures remains to be seen.

NOTES

1. A recent simple but useful overview of the Common Agricultural Policy is contained in John S. Marsh and Pamela J. Swanney, Agriculture and the European Community, Studies on Contemporary Europe

No. 2: George Allen & Unwin, London, 1980. A more detailed description is that by Rosemary Fennell, The Common Agricultural Policy of the European Community, Crosby Lockwood Staples, London, 1979. Theodore Heidhues, Tim Josling, Christopher Ritson and Stefan Tangermann, Thames Essay No. 14, TPRC, London, 1978 represents a good example of critical analysis of the CAP in recent years.

2.   These are the famous, or notorious, Article 39 objectives of the Treaty of Rome, which is the centrepiece of the series of Articles 38 to 47 which define the special position of agriculture within the European Economic Community.

3.   See, for example, Professors John S. Marsh and Christopher Ritson, Agricultural Policy and the Common Market, Chatham House/PEP European Series No. 16, 1971.

4.   See Heidhues et al (op. cit.)

5.   Fearn, H.A. and Irving, R.W., Green Money and the Common Agricultural Policy, Wye College, 1975.

6.   Directive 75/268 Mountain and Hill Farming and Farming in Certain Less Favourable Areas provides for special subsidies for agriculture in defined regions of the Community, particularly as part of farm development schemes, with the aim of helping the local economy and population to overcome natural disadvantages of climate, terrain or distance from markets.

7.   See Table 4.2 of Reflections on the Common Agricultural Policy, Commission of the European Communities, COM(80) 800 final, Brussels December 1980.

8.   See D. Gale Johnson, Food Reserves and International Trade Policy, Chapter 11 of: International Trade and Agriculture: theory and policy. ed. J.S. Hillman and A. Schmitz, Westfield Press, 1979.

9.   A number of studies of the internal and external effects of EC enlargement are available, e.g. J.M.C. Rollo 'The Second Enlargement of the European Economic Community' Journal of Agricultural Economics, Vol. 30(3), 1979. The 17th Report of the United Kingdom House of Lords Select Committee on the European Communities, Enlargement of the Community, Session 1977-78, HL 102, contains expert evidence on the subject.

Chapter 3

AN ECONOMIC FRAMEWORK

This chapter is concerned with developing a framework for measurement of the effects of the instruments of CAP, described in Chapter 2, on such groups
as producers, consumers and taxpayers and for the
measurement of the resulting inter-group and inter-
country transfers. The framework developed is a
simplification of the real world. It represents an
attempt to abstract the most important features of
the complexities of policy regulations and decision-
making in the agricultural market place. The model
can then be used to estimate the effects of changes
in agricultural policy on the groups of interest.
The credibility of the results depends, obviously,
on the structure of the model and the quality of the
data used in it.

The framework is developed in three dimensions:
commodities, countries, and groups within countries,
(namely: consumers, producers and taxpayers). The
instruments of CAP considered are: the common or
administered prices; import levies and export refunds; and Monetary Compensatory Accounts (MCAs).
Other instruments of the CAP are either ignored as
unchanging features outside the scope of the present
analysis or included only as accounting items. The
behaviour of consumers and producers is restricted
to the response in consumption and production levels
to changes in prices paid and received, while taxpayers enter the picture only as the group responsible in the last resort for Community budget surpluses and deficits resulting from the operation of
the CAP.

The next section of this chapter deals with the
basic economics of price support for individual
countries. This is extended to an economic ·commun-
ity in the following three sections by including,
respectively: community preference in agricultural
trade; country-differentiated prices for

agricultural commodities and the associated MCAs, and common financing of the community agricultural policy. The completed model is then summarised and the final section discusses important caveats and complications of the analysis.

THE ECONOMIC EFFECTS OF PRICE SUPPORT: THE SINGLE COUNTRY CASE

Economists use the ideas of supply and demand schedules to describe the behaviour of producers and consumers in response to price changes and to analyse the determination of prices and the effects of policies which manipulate prices. Figure 3.1a shows the conventional upward sloping supply curve S and downward sloping demand curve D, for a commodity and (importing) country of interest. These indicate that, at the price level Pw, domestic production would be Sw and domestic consumption Dw. The difference (Dw - Sw) is made up by imports, assuming, initially, that foreign supplies are available at price Pw and that any volume can be purchased at this price. If it is decided to support domestic prices at a higher level, Pc, then production would increase to Sc, consumption falls to Dc and imports fall to (Dc - Sc). Such a higher price could be achieved by imposing an import levy of (Pc - Pw) on all imports so that foreign goods could not undercut domestically produced goods selling at the new protected price Pc.

The extra production (Sc - Sw) over and above that called forth at the original price incurs additional costs which partly offset the extra revenue earned as a result of the higher price. Under certain conditions concerning the definition and specification of the supply curve, it is possible to assume that the supply curve shows, for each extra unit of output, the marginal costs of production. Thus area B + E, in Figure 3.1a, indicates the extra costs associated with the output (Sc - Sw), and the area A + B + E represents the increase in total revenue. The difference, area A, therefore represents the net gain to producers arising from the protection of the domestic industry, relative to net returns which would be earned under the old price Pw. Economists term this change in producer well being, producer surplus.

It should be noted however, that this gain may not always be retained by producers. To the extent that it makes production of this commodity more attractive than other lines of business, it will also increase demand for the fixed factors. Owners

of these factors may thus reap at least some of the
benefit conferred by the higher prices. In what
follows producer gain is thus used as a shorthand
for gains to owners of factors of production in
farming.

Consumers, or users of the commodity, on the
other hand, lose as a result of the move to the
higher price regime. Faced with a higher price they
buy less of the commodity. Their loss can be measured as area A + B + C + D in Figure 3.1a: economists refer to such areas as the change in consumer
surplus.[1] The rectangle A + B + C represents the
additional expenditure on quantity Dc. Triangle D
represents a measurement of the net loss which consumers experience as a result of consuming less,
since it measures the amount consumers would be
willing to pay in total over and above the old price,
Pw, to consume the extra quantity (Dw - Dc).

As a result of the import levy, the government
of the country raises a total revenue of the levy
(Pc - Pw) times the total quantity imported
(Dc - Sc), shown as area C in Figure 3.1a. This
gain to exchequer revenues over and above the previous position can be considered to accrue to taxpayers, as their tax burden can be reduced by an
equivalent amount, assuming that total government
expenditure is unchanged.

Provided that society values one unit (for
example £1 or 1DM) of producer benefit identically
with one unit of consumer loss and one unit of taxpayers gain, the gains and losses resulting from the
move to higher prices may be summed and the net gain
or loss to society determined. The result is shown
in the first column of Table 3.1.

An importing country suffers a net loss shown
by area B + D as a result of supporting prices at Pc
compared to Pw. In the economics literature this
loss is often called the "welfare cost" of price
support. An interpretation of the loss is that area
B represents the net cost of additional resources
withdrawn from the rest of the economy to support
the additional domestic production (Sc - Sw), which
could have been imported at price Pw. The area D is
the measure of the value of opportunities forgone by
consumers as a result of being required to pay price
Pc, rather than Pw. Areas B and D represent deadweight losses in the sense that they are not offset
by gain to any other group.

A similar analysis can be applied to an exporting country and this is shown in Figure 3.1b. The
results are summarized in the second column of
Table 3.1. The major difference from the importing

27

Table 3.1 : Gains and Losses from Price Support,
The Single Country Case.

		Importing Country	Exporting Country
Producer	Gain	A	(J + E + G)
Consumer	Loss	(A + B + C + D)	(J + E)
Taxpayer	Gain or Loss	C	(E + G + H)
Net Loss		(B + D)	(E + H)

(The letters refer to areas in Figures 3.1a
and 3.1b and denote sums of money.)

case arises from the fact that, in order to protect
a higher domestic price of Pc compared to Pw, an exporting country must remove the surplus of production over consumption at this price, (Sc - Dc). The
most economical method, from the point of view of
taxpayers, is to subsidize the export of the surplus
to the rest of the world. The necessary unit subsidy (or refund) is (Pc - Pw). The alternative of
buying up the surplus and either storing or destroy-
ing it will be more expensive under the assumption
that nothing else changes, i.e. that supply and
demand conditions do not alter.[2] The government
exchequer cost is E + G + H (Figure 3.1b) which is
the total value of export refunds necessary to
support the price of Pc rather than allow it to
remain at Pw.

As a first step in applying this analysis to
the price support system in the EC, the high domestic price level Pc can be thought of as the common
threshold price. In principle each member country
applies the same level of threshold prices and to
ensure imports do not undermine community prices at
or above this level, variable import levies are
charged on extra-community imports. Thus any
commodity offered at Pw is charged a levy of
(Pc - Pw) to bring it up to the common price level
Pc.

There are, in addition, two features of the
Community system of price support which distinguish
it from similar price support systems operating in a
single country. These are Community preference and
common financing.

FIGURE 3.1 THE ECONOMICS OF PRICE SUPPORT: THE SINGLE COUNTRY CASE

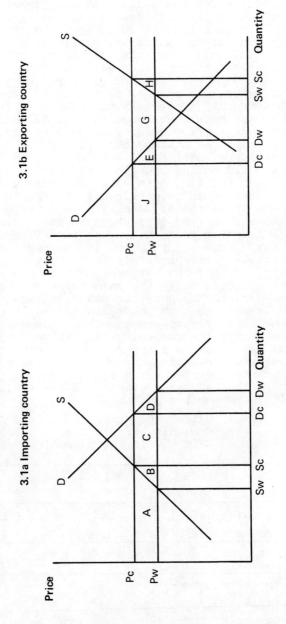

3.1a Importing country

3.1b Exporting country

COMMUNITY PREFERENCE

Community preference means that when trade occurs between two members it does so at the common price level Pc rather than at world prices with import levies and export subsidies. Referring back to Figure 3.1, this means that on imports which one country obtains from other members of the Community there are no import levies. In terms of the transfer involved, the part of area C corresponding to intra-Community trade does not accrue to the exchequer as import levy receipts but is paid by the consumer in the importing country directly to producers in the exporting country. By the same token, the export refunds (E + G + H in Figure 3.1b) are not required on that portion of exports destined for other members, since those members have undertaken to pay the common price directly to the exporters.

The operation of Community preference therefore changes the welfare sums shown in Table 3.1. Part of the taxpayer gain, C, in the importing country will now accrue to producers in the rest of the Community. Correspondingly in the exporting country, part of the taxpayer cost (E + G + H) will now be avoided, since the gain to producers is generated directly by sales to other members of the Community at the high protected prices. In the extreme case of just two countries for which, at the common price, the Community is just self sufficient, all of the trade is intra-Community trade at the common price and so all of area C is now a trade cost to the importer which exactly equals the trade gains in the exporting country (E + G + H). This result is summarised in Table 3.2.

Table 3.2 : Gains and Losses from Price Support and Community Preference: The Two Country, Self Sufficient Community Case.

	Importing Country	Exporting Country
Producer Gain	A	(J + E + G)
Consumer Loss	(A + B + C + D)	(J + E)
Net Loss or Gain	(B + C + D)	G
Trade Transfer:		
expenditure	C	
receipt		(E + G + H)

COMMON FINANCING

Common financing means that the Community is collectively responsible for paying for all aspects of market support under the CAP including the export refunds and MCA subsidies* incurred on trade in CAP products. It also means that levy revenue raised on imports from the rest of the world do not accrue to the importing country but are passed directly as own resources to the Community budget (although 10 per cent is deducted by the importing country to cover administrative costs). Similarly, MCA taxes* are also paid to the Community budget.

The common financing principle is fundamental to the concept of a <u>common</u> agricultural policy within a <u>community</u>. Without it there would be an incentive for importing countries to try and obtain supplies from the rest of the world and keep the import levies rather than purchasing at high prices from within the Community. Also, without common financing, importers could avoid sharing the budgetary burden of financing export refunds arising from other members exports to the rest of the world.

Budget transactions consequent on common financing further complicate the international and inter-group transfers resulting from the CAP. On trade with third countries the budget is credited with import levies but has to pay for export refunds. The balance of these credits and payments is the overall cost of market support. This balance is, of course, a deficit and is financed by contributions to the budget from the member states (the VAT based contributions). Policy changes which affect total net expenditures under the CAP therefore also affect the size of the VAT contribution required to finance the deficit. These contributions, therefore, should be included in any assessment of the economic impact of changes in CAP.

DIFFERENTIATED PRICES

Although one of the founding principles of the CAP was that there should be a common price applying in each member country for each commodity covered by the policy, for most of the 1970s price levels for the same commodity have differed substantially between member countries.[3] Unimpeded trade tends to equalise prices (apart from transport costs) between trading partners, raising domestic prices in the

---

* The next section explains these Monetary Compensatory Amounts.

exporting country as available supplies are reduced
by exports, and lowering those in importing countries by increasing available supplies. To protect
divergent domestic prices and yet still allow relatively free trade between member states a system of
border taxes and subsidies known as monetary compensatory amounts, MCAs, was introduced. These taxes
and subsidies are paid to and from the European
budget respectively, under the common financing
principle rather than accounted for by national exchequers.

The simplest way of understanding the prinsiple
of MCAs is to consider the taxes and subsidies in
relation to the common price, and treat trade as
occurring at this common price denominated in a
common currency. This is explained first for trade
within the community.

The system is illustrated in Figure 3.2 for
three countries: Country 1 has a lower domestic
price, P_1, than the common price, Pc, and has a
negative MCA; Country 2 has the domestic price, P_2,
at the common level and Country 3 has a higher price,
P_3, and a positive MCA.

The MCA system of subsidies and taxes does not
affect Country 2, whose trading price is the same as
the domestic price. In order to prevent prices in
Country 1 from rising towards common levels as trade
occurs intra-community imports must receive an MCA
subsidy of S_1. Thus importers can be thought of as
paying Pc at the border for imports and then receiving a subsidy of S_1 to allow those imports to compete on the domestic market. Exporters in Country 1,
however, must pay a tax of T_1 on their exports,
otherwise they would undermine the higher prices being maintained in the rest of the Community. Similarly, importers in Country 3 are required to pay a
tax T_3 on each unit they import and exporters receive a subsidy of S_3, both to protect the domestic
price level, P_3, and to enable exports to compete on
an equal basis in other member countries. In this
way the MCA system allows divergent price levels to
persist in the Community without being eroded by
trade flows.

As far as trade with the rest of the world is
concerned, protection of the common price, Pc, requires that import levies and export refunds equal
to (Pc - Pw) must be applied. With differentiated
prices, MCAs are added to, or subtracted from the
common levies or refunds. For example, Country 1
imports from the rest of the world bear the common
import levy (Pc - Pw) but receive an MCA subsidy of
S_1. Country 3 imports from the rest of the world

32

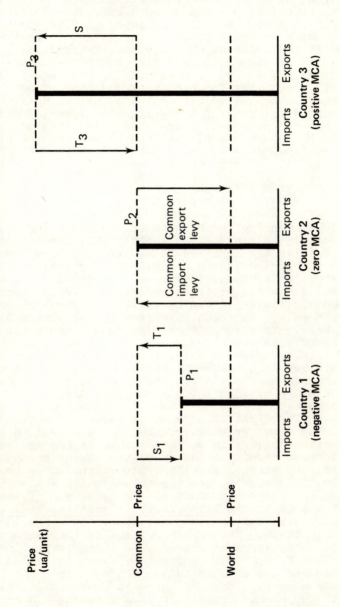

FIGURE 3.2 SCHEMATIC REPRESENTATION OF MONETARY COMPENSATORY AMOUNTS

33

bear both the common levy and the MCA tax of T3 to
bring up the price of these imports from Pw to P3.
In practice, MCA taxes and subsidies are netted
out of export refunds and import levies applying to
trade with the rest of the world and there are complicated rules about which country pays taxes and
which country gets subsidies on intra-community
trade. These rules present some problems in correc-
tly accounting for budgetary and other flows between
the member states but this need not be detailed
here.[4] In terms of the welfare analysis, providing
that the appropriate domestic price level (P_1 or P_3)
in the above example is substituted for the price
labelled Pc in the diagrams 3.1a and b, the previous
analysis is unchanged.[5]

SUMMARY OF TRANSFERS ARISING FROM
THE OPERATION OF THE CAP

To synthesise the results of the foregoing sections
for all possible cases (countries, commodities,
positive and negative MCAs, exporters and importers)
would be tedious, complicated and repetitive. However it is useful to show a simplified example of
how community preference, differentiated prices and
common financing can be built into the simple one-
commodity, two-country-community case described
above. This is done in Figure 3.3a and b and the
associated Table 3.3.
      In Figure 3.3a the total imports M have been
divided into intra-EC imports MI and extra-community
imports ME. Similarly the exports, X, in Figure
3.3b are divided into intra-, XI, and extra-, XE,
exports.
      The first three rows of Table 3.3 show the
trade flows arising from the operation of the
present policy in which domestic prices are Pc'.
Intra-community trade is valued at the common price,
Pc, and extra-community trade at the world price,
Pw, in order to show the values which would appear
in the current account of the Balance of Payments.
Row 3 shows the balance of agricultural trade. The
next six rows show the budgetary flows arising from
this trade. The export refunds on extra-community
exports represent expenditure in the exporting countries from FEOGA. Import levies on extra-community
imports are a contribution to FEOGA from the importing country. Each of these is measured in relation
to the common price. The MCAs, required because of
differentiated prices, are shown separately in row
6. In this example both are payments to FEOGA from
the member states. The eighth row shows the sum of

these budgetary flows for each member and this is
termed net FEOGA expenditure.

The total expenditure by the Community on guarantees and subsidies for all agricultural commodities, net of levy income, shown in row 9 represents
a budgetary cost to be met from other sources through
a financial mechanism of some kind. There are a
number of possible ways this expenditure could be
allocated to each member-state. Row 9 shows it made
up by VAT contributions using the shares α and $1 - \alpha$
which occurred under the base policy, since it is
these contributions which comprise the marginal form
of financing the CAP as the policy's net expenditure
changes. The balance of Community expenditures and
these VAT contributions for each national government
or intervention agency, row 10, may be termed the
balance of FEOGA payments for the country concerned.
This represents the net balance of official or
budgetary flows across the exchanges which arise
through participation in the CAP.

An overall balance of agricultural payments for
each EC member, row 11, is the sum of the 'public'
balance of FEOGA payments and the 'private' balance
of agricultural trade, valued, as explained above,
at world or Community price levels according to the
trading partner concerned. The balance of agricultural payments represents the contribution to the
national balance of payments made by all flows
arising from agricultural trade under the CAP.
Changes in the CAP or its method of finance will
have consequences for both physical trade in affected commodities and/or on the flows of payments between national governments and the Community. The
net effect of such changes on national balances of
payments will be of greater or lesser interest
according to the macro-economic concerns in member
states. In addition these balance of payments
effects are bound up with other Community arrangements such as the European Monetary System (EMS),
but such interactions are beyond the scope of this
study.

Each of the trade and payments balances referred to above may be measured uniquely for any
given policy situation. However, none can be taken
as a suitable measure of the effective cost (or
benefit) of the policy to a member country, since
the negative (or positive) balance would not necessarily disappear if the policy were abandoned by
that country. From the point of view of the present
study of the costs of the CAP, it is the change in
these balances and in other measures, such as price
levels, when moving from a base CAP position to some

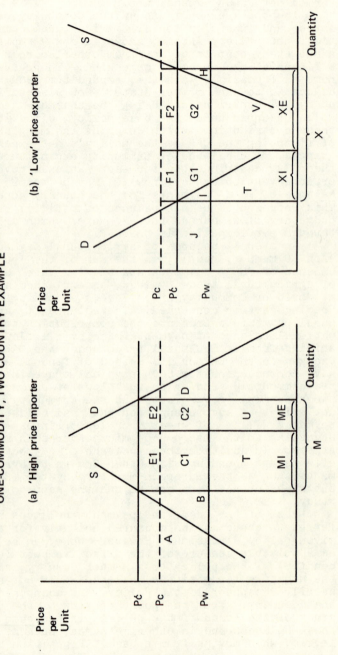

FIGURE 3.3 TRANSFERS ARISING FROM THE OPERATION OF THE CAP: ONE-COMMODITY, TWO COUNTRY EXAMPLE

(a) 'High' price importer

(b) 'Low' price exporter

TABLE 3.3 : Summary of Transfers in a Two-country Community

	(a) High price importer	(b) Low price exporter
Trade Flows:		
1. Export receipts		$T+V+G_1+F_1+I$
2. Import payments	$T+U+C_1$	
3. Balance of Agric. Trade (1+2)	$-(T+U+C_1)$	$T+V+G_1+F_1+I$
Budgetary Flows:		
4. Export refunds		gain F_2+G_2+H
5. Import levies	loss C_2	loss F_1+F_2
6. MCAs	loss E_1+E_2	
7. Net FEOGA expenditure (4+5+6)	loss $C_2+E_1+E_2$	gain G_2+H-F_1
8. Total community expenditure	$(G_2+H) -$	$(F_1+C_2+E_1+E_2) = Z$
9. VAT contributions ($\alpha 8$)	loss αZ	loss $(1-\alpha)Z$
10. Balance of FEOGA payments (7+9)	loss $C_2+E_1+E_2+\alpha Z$	gain $G_2+H-F_1-(1-\alpha)Z$
11. Balance of Agric. payments (10+3)	loss $C_2+E_1+E_2+\alpha Z+T+U+C_1$	gain $G_2+H+T+V+G_1-(1-\alpha)Z+I$
12. Preferential trade effect	loss C_1	gain $I+G_1+F_1$
13. Budget and trade effect (10+12)	loss $C_1+C_2+E_1+E_2+\alpha Z$	gain $I+G_1+G_2+H-(1-\alpha)Z$
Welfare Effects:		
14. Producers	gain A	gain $J+I+G_1+G_2$
15. Consumers	loss $A+B+C_1+C_2+E_1+E_2+D$	loss $J+I$
16. Taxpayers	loss αZ	loss $(1-\alpha)Z$
17. Overall welfare	loss $B+C_1+C_2+E_1+E_2+D+\alpha Z$	gain $G_1+G_2-(1-\alpha)Z$

specified alternative that properly reflects the
opportunity loss or gain of CAP membership.

One such alternative is to assume that a single
country withdraws from the CAP yet maintains domestic
prices at existing levels, and trades in all agricultural products at (unchanged) world prices by means
of national export subsidies and import levies.
Under these rather strict assumptions, quantities
produced, consumed and traded in the withdrawing
country remain unchanged (since net prices are unaltered), but the balances of trade and payments are
affected. In particular, there would normally be
losses in foreign exchange incurred on selling exports of agricultural products to other EC members
at world rather than EC prices, and corresponding
gains on preferential imports. In terms of Figure
3.3, row 12 shows such an effect vis-a-vis this specific alternative to the CAP, here termed the preferential trade effect. In the case of the importing
country, the effect of maintaining high EC price
levels for intra-community trade constitutes a loss
of foreign exchange which appears as an equivalent
gain to its exporting partner. To the preferential
trade effect may be added the balance of FEOGA payments to or from the Community under CAP, including
the financial contribution. The result is called the
budget and trade effect, row 13, and represents the
overall balance of payments effect of moving from the
CAP to a national rather than a common policy, while
keeping domestic price levels unchanged.

The budgetary and trade flows and balances
above arise from the operation of the CAP as it
affects each member of the Community. As such,
these flows, and changes in them under alternative
systems, are of direct and obvious concern to
national governments. However, welfare effects of
policy changes are represented by the gains and losses to producers and consumers of the type described
in the single-country case above. These are shown
in rows 14 and 15 of Figure 3.3 for the extreme case
of a move from the CAP to free trade at world price
levels. In addition to producer and consumer
effects, taxpayers would then be relieved of the
burden of financing the policy, row 16, and the
overall welfare effect is the sum of these three
items, row 17. In the example shown in Figure and
Table 3.3 the losses to consumers and taxpayers ex-
ceed the gains to producers in the importing country.
In the exporting country the gains to producers
may outweigh the losses to consumers and taxpayers
depending on the comparative magnitude between
the members of the community of: trade with

the rest of the world, the size of MCAs, the shares
of Community VAT contributions, and the responsiveness of supply and demand.*
    Whilst subject to a number of important simpli-
fications discussed below, Table 3.3 shows that
there are a number of quite different concepts of
the 'cost' of CAP to a member country. Rows 3, 7, 9,
10, 11, 13, and 14 to 17 are all intrinsically interesting as indicators of aspects of the cost of the
CAP. Chapter 4 discusses the literature on costs of
the CAP showing that much of the attention has been
restricted to just two of these costs, the budget
and trade effect (row 13). Yet another measure of
cost, which on its own has little theoretical merit,
was the subject of considerable political attention
in the United Kingdom in 1979/80, namely the net
budgetary flow, the sum of rows 7 and 9, labelled in
the popular press as "Mrs. Thatcher's Billion".
    The remaining sections of this chapter discuss
various further considerations and qualifications
which should be borne in mind when interpreting the
results of calculations using the economic framework
above, whether in the work of others (Chapter 4) or
in the present study (Chapters 5 to 9).

ALTERNATIVE POLICIES

A guiding principle of economic analysis is that
there is no such thing as an absolute cost. The
cost of anything can only be measured in terms of
what has to be given up to achieve it, that is, the
cost relative to some alternative. In matters of
individual or business choice the true cost of an
action is the relative gain from the best alternative action from the set of those known to the
decision-maker. In the context of the choice of
supra-national agricultural policy there is an extremely large set of alternatives and the choice of
which is 'best' is based to a large extent on political as well as economic criteria. Thus there is no
single opportunity cost of the CAP but a number of
different costs arising from possible alternative
policies.

---

* The reader should recall that the convention used
  here is that the current position is being compared
  to an alternative policy (e.g. free trade). If
  this change helps a group,(e.g. consumers) by lowering prices, then the current situation <u>costs</u>
  consumers by the appropriate amount.

The range of such alternatives is wide. Two possible criteria for selecting particular ones for analysis are political feasibility and computational ease. In this study four policy changes are analysed: (i) a particular price package agreed by the Council of Ministers; (ii) the elimination of MCAs; (iii) the achievement of self-sufficiency within the Community and (iv) to move to free trade with the rest of the world. Compared to most of the alternatives used by previous researchers, as described in the following chapter, all of these are computationally difficult. The first alternative is obviously politically feasible (and in fact is of a type implemented each year), the second less so but nevertheless still included in statements of policy goals by responsible Community interests. The third is included less because many politicians espouse it than for its demonstration of how the budgetary problem is 'solved' by self-sufficiency. The fourth is not politically feasible but it has an intellectual appeal and is frequently used by economists as a bench mark for measuring costs, benefits and transfers.[6]

PARTIAL, COMPARATIVE-STATIC ANALYSIS

The analysis in this study is restricted to the effects of the price support system of the CAP. The interrelationships between this part of the CAP and the smaller structural policy component of the CAP have been ignored. Also ignored are: the effects of high food prices on consumer expenditure elsewhere in the economy; the effects of producer support on ancillary agribusiness; the effects of flows of money between member states on exchange rates and the subsequent effects on economic activity in the member states. In the economist's jargon the analysis is partial rather than general. A more general analysis would require not only considerably more work and effort, but also additional restrictions, assumptions and simplifications, many of which would be subject to further caveats. It is doubtful if much greater insight into the CAP would be gained by formally including such wider considerations into the analysis, but naturally they can and should be taken into account when arriving at an overall judgement of the quantitative results.

Not only is the framework used in the study partial, but it also employs the technique of comparative statics. That is, attention is devoted to the differences in the levels of variables (trade flows, prices, budgetary flows, etc.) between a base position and the alternative. No light can therefore be shed on the adjustment processes involved in reactions to changes in CAP. In particular no indication is given of the time taken for economic agents to adjust fully to changes in policy signals. The results discussed in Chapters 6 to 9 below represent the long run equilibrium effects of changes in policy. This again causes difficulties at the interpretative stage.

WORLD PRICE EFFECTS

For many commodities, particularly those in which the Community is more than self-sufficient, the EC is a relatively large trader in world markets. The amount which the Community exports and imports from the rest of the world is likely to have some impact on world prices. For any policy change which alters the level of imports and exports with the rest of the world, this could be important as it changes the unit values of import levies and export refunds. This 'terms of trade' effect complicates the analysis above because it requires the relationship between EC export levels and world prices to be included. However, qualitatively, the general framework of the analysis still applies. Recognition of the 'terms of trade' effect means, for instance, that the effect of increasing common prices would be both to increase the EC exportable surplus and to decrease world prices (thus increasing the unit export refund), and so in two ways to increase the total expenditure on export refunds. To the extent that some member countries continue to import from the rest of the world, the unit levies increase and the total levies collected may increase or decrease.

SURPLUS DISPOSAL COSTS

A simplification that has been made so far is that any excess of production over consumption at EC price levels is exported to the world market, using export refunds to allow such exports to be competitive with supplies from elsewhere in the world. In fact the Community also buys up surpluses from time to time and places them in intervention stores; it subsidises Community consumption or processing of some commodities. These are all intended to relieve the market of surplus production and thus support market prices. All of these programmes result in some budget expenditure, which may or may not be equivalent, on a per unit basis, to the cost of export refunds. It is important therefore to consider whether treatment of all surplus as if it were exported biases total budget expenditure, and if so, whether these other programmes should be included separately in the analysis.

The decision to place some surplus production in intervention storage results in charges to the EC budget for physical storage costs and interest charges on the value of the stock. The budget also bears the annual carrying charge on any stock carried over from previous years. From an economic point of view, the costs associated with previous years' surpluses are more properly associated with those previous years rather than the current year, and by the same token, the commitment to future years' expenditure that is implied by storing this year's surplus should properly count as part of this year's costs. Since intervention and subsidised private storage only delay budget expenditure on disposal of surpluses on the world market, rather than avoiding them altogether, the simplest solution is to charge surpluses as if they were all exported.7 This will, however, yield a different, and probably higher, budgetary cost than the one contained in the published budget accounts. Consumer and processing subsidies are applied as a safety valve on burgeoning intervention stocks, and also for other social and political reasons. They can be included directly in the analysis by making the appropriate distinction between producer and consumer, or user, prices.

CROSS-PRICE EFFECTS ON SUPPLY AND DEMAND

A further simplification of the above analysis is to treat the supply and demand of each commodity as if these quantities were unaffected by changes in the prices of other commodities covered by the CAP. However, these "cross-price" effects can be significant, particularly in the case of intermediate or competitive products; for example, the price of cereals affects the supply of pork and poultry, and the price of beef affects the supply of milk. Inclusion of cross-price elasticities which quantify such impacts is likely to be important in analysing the changes which would occur when the prices of many commodities covered by the CAP are changed simultaneously. When they are included, however, it does create a problem for the correct measurement of consumer and producer effects. This point is taken up in Chapter 5.

ADDITIVITY OF TRANSFERS, COSTS AND BENEFITS

Several different types of transfer have been identified in this chapter, including producer gains,
consumer and taxpayer losses, budgetary flows and
trade-cost flows. In Table 3.3 these transfers
were combined to calculate an overall indicator of
economic welfare. This is a legitimate procedure
only if certain conditions hold, most importantly
any monetary amount lost by one group is judged by
society to be equivalent to the same amount lost by
any other group. Without this assumption distributional weights would be necessary in order to assess
the welfare effects for society as a whole of a
given change in policy.

INTRA-COMMUNITY TRADE

A final qualification of the framework summarised in
this chapter concerns the determination of intra-
community trade flows and in particular how these
respond to changes in policy. Throughout the
analysis transport costs are ignored; thus there is
no spatial price differentiation per se. Together
with the common policy price (at least for trade,
after compensation by MCAs) throughout the Community,
this begs the question of what signals determine the
pattern of intra-EC trade. With many countries in
the Community there is the further problem of allocating the intra-EC trade amongst members. This is
an area requiring considerable research, since it
does not appear to have been addressed in the
literature to date though it clearly involves difficult problems of data consistency and model formulation.

NOTES

1.   In this agricultural context, to avoid confus-
ion over the word surplus, the terms producer and
consumer 'surplus' will not be used. Instead the
words 'effect', 'gain' or 'loss' will be used.

2.   This trade-off between alternative methods of
disposing of excess supplies is discussed in some
detail in Buckwell and Harvey (1981) for the EC
policy, see note 5 below.

3.   The origin of differentiated prices was the
divergence of member state currencies as a result of
exchange rate changes in the late sixties and the
collapse of the Bretton Woods system of fixed

exchange rates in the early seventies. As the
prices at which CAP products are supported are denominated in units of account (UAs), exchange rate
changes between member state currencies and the UA
causes prices in member state currencies to change.
For the purposes of this paper the genesis of
differentiated prices is less important than their
effects. The reader interested in the development
of MCAs, and associated changes in definition of the
unit of account is referred to Irving, R.W. and
Fearn, H.A., Green Money and the Common Agricultural
Policy, Wye College, 1975; Heidhues, T., Josling,
T.E., Ritson, C. and Tangermann, S., Common Prices
and Europe's Farm Policy, Trade Policy Research
Centre, Thames Essay, 1978; Ritson C., and Tangermann, S., "The Economics and Politics of Monetary
Compensatory Amounts", European Review of Agricultural Economics, Vol. 6(1), 1979, pp 119-164. In
effect, however, the development has meant that individual countries price levels have diverged substantially from the common price level at market
exchange rates. The MCA percentage applying to a
particular country (and commodity) at a particular
point of time is a measure of this divergence. The
United Kingdom's MCA has been as low as -45% (United
Kingdom prices below common price levels) in late
1976 and as high as +18% in early 1981. Germany's
MCA has been consistently positive since 1970
(domestic German support prices being above Community
levels) by between +7.5% and +12.03%. While no
other country has had the same extent of MCA experience as the United Kingdom, other MCAs have also
changed from time to time. The previous history of
MCAs and associated green rates of exchange is doc-
umented in the CAP Monitor, Agra Europe (London)
Ltd.

4.   The general rule, since mid-1973, has been that
each member state is responsible for the initial
collection or final distribution of its own MCA
taxes and subsidies respectively, that is, the practical analogue of the principle described in the
text. However, because of some financial advantage
deriving from outdated monetary parities to the
European budget, it was agreed in May 1976 that the
total MCA subsidies payable on imports into the
United Kingdom and Italy (then with negative MCAs)
should be paid to the exporting country (the so-
called "exporter-pays" system). This system is,
however, only applicable to the payment of negative
MCAs and has thus been suspended in favour of the
general rule for the United Kingdom since the

emergence of a positive MCA (due to appreciation of the pound sterling against other currencies and the EUA) in mid 1980. For further details of the practice of MCA payments and reference to the appropriate EC regulations the reader is referred to Agra Europe, CAP Monitor (op. cit.) Chapter 2.

5.   In much public discussion of the budgetary flows arising from the operation of the CAP the question of to whom MCAs are paid has been identified as an important issue. However, provided the analyst accounts for all the effects of the protected and differentiated prices in the Community as outlined in Figure 3.1 and Table 3.1, and not just the budgetary effects, then the institutional arrangements for the payment of MCAs is not important.

6.   The reasons for this choice have to do with the results of such a system in distributing income among the members of society and making the best use of all available resources (land, labour and capital) to produce according to the needs of society, as expressed by the willingness to pay. Under a perfectly competitive market system, it turns out that it is not possible to make any one individual or group better off without making someone worse off. Needless to say, as with many economic propositions, there is considerable debate about the content and relevance of this theory.

7.   For a more complete justification for this approach, see Buckwell, A.E., and Harvey, D.R., "Market Variability and the CAP : a neglected area?". Section III.1 of Consideration and modelling of risk in the Agribusiness Sector, C.-Hennig Hanf and Gerhard Scheifer (eds.) Kieler Wissenschaftsverlag Vautg Kiel, 1981.

Chapter 4

SURVEY AND SYNTHESIS OF PREVIOUS WORK

The literature relating to the 'costs' of the Common
Agricultural Policy falls into two broad categories.
First there are studies which attempt to measure the
costs of the existing policy against an alternative
which is radically different. The second category
contains studies which evaluate marginal changes in
the CAP

STUDIES MEASURING THE BUDGET
AND TRADE EFFECTS OF CAP

All the studies examined in this section divide the
cost of the CAP between member countries, and except
for Blancus, 1978[1], provide a breakdown by commodity.
Each emphasises different aspects of these costs,
however, and important provisos must be kept in mind
when comparing them. Nevertheless, each essentially
calculates a cost similar to the Budget and Trade
Effect outlined in Chapter 3.

Institute for Fiscal Studies The study for the
Institute of Fiscal Studies (IFS) by Morris[2] uses a
framework similar to that outlined in Chapter 3.
His model covers 17 commodities, viz: durum wheat,
common wheat, barley, rye, oats, maize, cheese,
sugar, butter, powdered milk, beef, pigmeat, rice,
eggs, poultry, olive oil, and milk. In order to
measure consumer and producer effects and the budgetary transfers, official statistics on production,
consumption and average selling prices in member
countries are combined with own price elasticities
of demand and supply from previous studies, and
Morris' own estimates of world prices. The calculations mostly follow the conventions described in
Chapter 3, in particular all surplus being disposed
of through subsidised exports.
       Three main points should be made with respect to

the data on elasticities. First, it is derived from many different sources[3] and inconsistencies may be present. This was circumvented by assuming that the elasticity for each commodity is the same in all countries. Second, where little significant information is available and elasticity of $\pm$ 0.3 is assumed, this applied to eighteen of thirty four cases. Third, the IFS study does not include cross-price elasticities. Thus, in order to allow for the effect of prices of related commodities moving together, the initial model estimates of consumer losses for cereals, meat and milk products, and all producer gains are halved to reflect the inter-dependence between products.

Considerable attention was given in the IFS study to the estimation of a reasonable world price, required in the calculations. Despite the thoroughness of this investigation, an inconsistency appears to have arisen. Several adjustments are made in arriving at world prices, one of which is to assume that in the situation without the CAP the different member countries would establish different agricultural price levels, and that this, by affecting the supply-demand balance in each country, would affect world prices. Having obtained these adjusted world prices however, the different domestic policies seem to have been forgotten, because the cost of the CAP is determined by comparing the "with CAP" situation with a "without CAP" situation in which producer and consumer benefits in each country are measured at the adjusted world prices and not the prices that would prevail given the assumed domestic policies. Thus in the published results the consumer losses and producer gains in Germany and France are shown as substantial amounts. If agriculture were to be supported at about the same level with and without the CAP in these countries then only small consumer losses and producer gains would be expected from a removal of CAP.

Having measured consumer welfare losses and producer welfare gains, the third part of the IFS analysis is to include the budget cost. This is defined for each country by applying the proportion of total EC expenditure devoted to agriculture to each country's payment of customs duties and VAT. The sum of the changes in consumer and producer welfare plus the budget cost is termed the effect on resources, that is, an overall measure of net welfare, see Chapter 3.

The country breakdown of the IFS analysis on the cost of the CAP is shown in Table 4.1. The results chiefly apply to 1978, but an additional side calculation yields a single row of figures for the expected position of the United Kingdom in 1980 showing an effect on resources of -£2355.

Table 4.1 : Costs of the CAP :
              Institute of Fiscal Studies

				(1978, £ million)
Country	Con-sumer Loss**	Pro-ducer Gain*	Budgetary Contri-bution	Effect on Re-sources
Germany	4598	4035	1177	-1740
France	3167	3642	761	-286
Italy	3413	2257	386	-1541
Netherlands	892	1403	305	+206
Belgium	725	680	226	-259
United Kingdom	1787	1148	731	-1370
Ireland	175	408	32	+201
Denmark	291	713	117	+324
(Subsidies unallo-cated to countries)(-7)				
(Restitutions and subsidies on pro-ducts not covered)			(-380)	
EC Total:	15041**	14286*	3357	-4112
United Kingdom 1980	2813	1558	1050	-2355

*   Includes Guidance Section Payments.

**   After allowing for subsidies.

SOURCE : Morris "The Common Agricultural Policy"
         Fiscal Studies 1,(2), pp.17-35

49

Cambridge Economic Policy Group   The Cambridge
Economic Policy Group (CEPG) have produced a series
of estimates of the costs of the CAP[4], all of which
concentrate on the Budget and Trade Effect discussed
in Chapter 3. The results are given by country, but
only seven commodities are covered, viz: barley,
wheat, maize, sugar, butter, cheese and beef. In a
similar way to the Institute for Fiscal Studies, the
CEPG compare a situation with the CAP in full operation with one in which intra- and extra-EC trade
takes place at world prices and member states continue their existing levels of support but finance
them independently rather than jointly.

    There are several methodological differences
between the CEPG analyses of the cost of the CAP and
that completed by the IFS. Firstly the Cambridge
team, instead of dividing the cost into the three
components - consumer loss, producer gain and budget
cost - use the two cost components: net budget
costs and net trade costs. The former includes all
receipts and payments for individual countries with
the EC budget. Thus, refunds and levies, which in
the IFS analysis form part of producer gains and
consumer losses, are now included in the budget
item. Net trade costs are a measure of the effect
of valuing intra-EC trade at world prices rather
than at member country domestic prices. The second
difference between the IFS and CEPG analyses is that
because no price changes are envisaged in the CEPG
analysis, supply and demand responses are ignored.
However despite the differences in methodology of
the IFS and the Cambridge group, it can be shown
that because domestic prices are assumed not to
change they should obtain similar results if their
input data is the same.

    The CEPG analysis included all items in the
budget, both agricultural and non-agricultural.
This means that an overestimate of the costs of the
CAP alone would be expected. Another difficulty is
that there appears to be a double counting of MCAs.
They are certainly included in the net budget
receipts and payments, and the different national
price levels used in the calculation of net trade
costs imply they are also included there. The
results of the CEPG evaluation of the costs of the
CAP for 1979 are shown in Table 4.2.

Table 4.2 : Net Cash Receipts and Payments Between EC Members : CEPG

(1979, £ million)

Country	Net Budget Receipt	Net Trade Receipt	Total Net Cash Receipt
United Kingdom	-806	-317	-1123
Germany	-570	-101	-671
Italy	-114	-532	-646
Belgium-Luxembourg	+312	-156	+156
Ireland	+254	+221	+475
Holland	+190	+441	+631
Denmark	+329	+289	+618
France	+114	+620	+734

SOURCE : Cambridge Economic Policy Group, "Policies of the EEC", Chapter 2
Cambridge Economic Policy Review, Gower Press, Cambridge, 1979.

Rollo and Warwick[5] A Government Economic Service
(GES) working paper by two officials of the Ministry
of Agriculture, Fisheries and Food (MAFF), Rollo and
Warwick, shows a similar calculation to the CEPG but
avoiding the double counting of MCA payments. The
alternative policy for comparison is the same as
that chosen by the CEPG, that is agricultural
support in each member country at the current CAP
levels, but financed by the individual countries.
This implies no change in the quantities produced,
consumed or traded.

Apart from the treatment of MCAs, noted above,
there are several differences in detail between the
Rollo and Warwick and CEPG analyses. First, the net
budget cost item includes only estimated expenditure
and income related to the CAP. Second, two options
are presented for deriving world prices: EC common
prices less import levies, and common prices less
export refunds. Hence two sets of results are produced. Another difference is that more commodities
are included: rice, pigmeat, poultrymeat and eggs
are added, and wheat is disaggregated into common
wheat and durum wheat. The analysis was applied to
the two years 1977 and 1978, the results for 1978
are shown in Table 4.3.

Table 4.3 : Effect of the CAP on the Balance of Payments of Member States: Rollo and Warwick.

(1978, £ million)

	Belg/Lux.	Den.	Ger.	France	Ire.	Italy	Neth.	U.K.
Gross contributions to FEOGA	394	137	1858	1153	35	860	615	920
Gross receipts from FEOGA	427	345	1736	1194	378	516	856	247
Net receipt (+) from or contribution (-) to FEOGA	+33	+408	-122	+41	+343	-344	+241	-673
Benefits of higher export prices as measured by:								
(a) import levies	408	287	458	997	238	54	926	273
(b) export restitutions	287	222	366	801	211	45	653	283
Cost of higher import prices as measured by:								
(a) import levies	462	12	892	422	54	926	321	383
(b) export restitutions	382	9	648	321	48	487	266	428
Net effect on trade account:								
(a) at import levies	-54	+275	-434	+575	+184	-588	+605	-110
(b) at export restitutions	-95	+213	-282	+480	+163	-442	+387	-145
Net effect on balance of payments								
(a) at import levies	-21	+683	-556	+616	+527	-932	+846	-783
(b) at export restitutions	-62	+621	-404	+521	+506	-786	+628	-818

SOURCE : Rollo and Warwick, "The CAP and Resource Flows Among EEC Member States", Government Service Working Paper No. 27. Ministry of Agriculture, Fisheries and Food, London, 1979.

53

Koester[6] Professor U. Koester of the University of
Kiel utilizes essentially the same method in his
study as the CEPG and Rollo and Warwick, except that
he does not provide a breakdown into trade and
budget cost, but merely shows the overall outcome.
The study covers six products: soft wheat, barley,
white sugar, beef and veal, butter and skim milk
powder; for five years 1971 to 1975; and for five
countries: Germany, France, Italy, Netherlands and
the United Kingdom. The present CAP financial system
is compared with a nationally financed agricultural
policy system in which all trade flows are valued at
world prices. The meagre details presented by
Koester about the methodology mean that little
further can be added here. The results for the most
recent year of the study, 1975, are shown in Table
4.4.

Table 4.4 : National Net Transfer Payments Due to the Common Organisation of Markets: Koester.

(1975, million ua)

Country	Soft Wheat	Barley	White Sugar	Beef and Veal	Butter	Skim Milk Powder	Sum(a)
1975							
F.R. Germany	6.549	14.443	-130.993	-49.900	106.644	22.720	-29.987
France	-46.217	-30.719	-158.527	100.789	60.261	23.629	-410.784
Italy	6.637	11.205	168.094	-301.942	-44.922	-41.812	-202.740
Netherlands	4.938	2.583	-74.624	37.024	153.392	-4.002	119.311
United Kingdom	23.040	5.798	708.691	-134.917	1393.951	-20.219	118.442

(a)   Sum of the products considered.

SOURCE : Koester, U. "The Redistributional Effects of the Common Agricultural Financial System". European Review of Agricultural Economics 4,(4) pp.321-345.

Blancus[7]   Using a similar framework as the CEPG,
Blancus calculates just the trade effect of intra-EC
trade omitting the budget receipts and payments.
The results cover seven of the nine member states,
with Ireland and Luxembourg omitted. The analysis
was completed for each year from 1970 to 1976 and
all CAP products were included. Aggregation of the
transfers from the consumers of each member country
to the farmers of other EC members and to the
Community budget, with the inflows of foreign exchange for each member country because of agricultural transfers to farmers from consumers in other
EC countries, yields the net gains and costs on
intra-EC trade as a result of the CAP shown in Table
4.5.

Table 4.5 : Net Gain (+) or Net Loss (-) Because of the CAP for the Balance of Payments of each Member Country : Blancus.

(million US Dollars)

Country	1970	1971	1972	1973	1974	1975	1976
Germany	-363	-467	-767	-424	-186	-231	-219
France	289	476	391	287	8	269	489
Italy	-845	-896	-1057	-1064	-741	-1182	-1325
Netherlands	93	143	82	77	218	142	164
Belgium	98	-30	-166	-70	-77	-203	-232
United Kingdom				-1861	-1768	-1524	-1067
Denmark				16	-37	32	-25

SOURCE : Blancus "The Common Agricultural Policy and the Balance of Payments of the EEC Member Countries". Quarterly Review of Banca Nazionale del Lauoro, 5, (3), pp.355-70.

COMPARISON OF STUDIES MEASURING BUDGET AND TRADE
EFFECTS OF CAP

Table 4.6 brings together estimates of the budget
and trade effect concept of the cost of the CAP
measured against the same policy alternative of
nationally financed agricultural support at existing
price levels without community preference from each
of the above five studies. The most obvious conclusion is that there are large differences between
the results, largely because of differences in years
and commodities covered, as well as methodology.
Perhaps this emphasises the fact that there is no
unique measure of the cost of the CAP. The 1978/79
results all show Germany, Italy and the United
Kingdom to be net losers from the CAP, with Belgium/
Luxembourg being a net loser in the three out of four
cases. The Netherlands, Ireland and Denmark are net
beneficiaries, with France being a net gainer in
three of the four studies.

TABLE 4.6 : A Comparison Between Studies Measuring the Costs of the CAP.

(£ million)

Country	Morris 1978	Cambridge 1979	Rollo and Warwick[a] 1978	Rollo and Warwick[b] 1978	Koester[c] 1975	Blancus[d] 1976
Germany	-1740	-671	-404	-556	+12	-122
France	-286	+734	+521	+616	+170	+272
Italy	-1541	-646	-786	-932	-85	-736
Netherlands	+206	+631	+628	+846	-50	+91
Belgium/Luxembourg	-259	+156	-62	-21		-129
United Kingdom	-1370	-1123	-818	-783	-79	-593
Ireland	+201	+475	+506	+527		
Denmark	+324	+618	+621	+683		-14

SOURCES: Morris, C.N., "The Common Agricultural Policy", Fiscal Studies, 1, (2) 1980, pp. 17-35.

Cambridge Economic Policy Group, "Policies of the EEC", Chapter 2 in Cambridge Economic Policy Review Vol. 15, Gower Press, Cambridge, 1979.

Rollo, J.N.C. and Warwick, K.S., "The CAP and Resource Flows Among EEC Member States", Government Economic Service Working Paper, No. 27, London.

Koester, U. "The Redistributional Effects of the Common Agricultural Financial System" European Review of Agricultural Economics, Vol. 4, (4), 1977, pp. 321-345.

Blancus, P. "The CAP and the Balance of Payments of the EEC Member Countries" Quarterly Review of Banca Nazionale del Lavoro, Vol. 5, (3), 1978, pp.355-370.

a.   With net effect on trade account measured using export restitutions.
b.   With net effect on trade account measured using import levies.
c.   Converted from units of account at 1 u.a. = £0.41667.
d.   Converted from $US at $1 = £0.55595.

Apart from this broad agreement on which countries are the losers and which the gainers, there is
little agreement on the magnitude of the gains or
losses. The IFS figures differ from those of the
CEPG and Rollo and Warwick studies in that the
losers all lose more and the gainers all gain less.
It is not possible to pin-point the entire source
of the discrepancies, but it may be a combination of
different measures of broadly the same concept of
cost, and different detailed assumptions (commodity
coverage, production, consumption and trade and
price data). The CEPG figures all lie outside the
range provided by the Rollo and Warwick figures.
The range of the estimates for each country is
£60-£300m which is about 10-40 per cent of the
average estimates. The discrepancies are greatest
for the large countries.
    The conclusion seems to be that estimates of the
budget and trade effect of the CAP compared to a
nationally financed version at current support levels should be assumed to have a fairly large margin
of error. This, together with the fact that the
alternative policy specified in these calculations
seems neither desirable (insofar as no significant
party is lobbying for it) nor likely (in that member
country support levels would almost certainly diverge from current levels under national policies)
suggests that analyses might be more usefully conducted of marginal changes in the CAP which are
actively being suggested. Such analyses are discussed in the next section.

MEASURING THE COST OF CHANGES IN THE CAP

Institute for Fiscal Studies[8] The IFS study, in
addition to calculating an overall cost of the CAP,
also analysed the effect on the United Kingdom of a
devaluation of the green pound and of an increase in
the selling price of the 17 agricultural commodities.
A one per cent devaluation of the green pound is
estimated to involve an overall net loss of £21.5
million (in 1978). This is comprised of consumer
losses of £62.0 million, producer gains of £36.8
million and a net reduction in Britain's contribution to the EC budget of £3.7 million. From this
result the effect of the five per cent devaluation
of the green pound which occurred in December 1979,
is extrapolated in the study to give a net cost to
the United Kingdom of about £100 million.

Cambridge Economic Policy Group[9] The CEPG also
represents an analysis of the effects of changes in

green rates in each of the Nine. Three possible
changes are analysed, viz: changes in all green
currencies to bring all prices to the common prices;
a movement in all green currencies to bring prices
to the German price level; and a movement in all
green currencies except those of the UK and Italy to
bring prices to the German level. Only the third
alternative is considered politically feasible by
the CEPG because the first two involved substantial
price increases in the United Kingdom and Italy,
and the first also involves price reductions for
farmers in Germany. The result of the upward harmonisation of prices in exporting countries to the
German level is, of course, a large increase in the
overall cost of CAP support which is paid for by the
importing countries, particularly the United Kingdom
and Germany, and benefiting the large exporters
especially France.

Koester[10]   Koester's main analysis is the estimation of the effects of a one per cent price rise in
the six agricultural commodities in his model. He
analyses the budget and trade effect of a one per
cent rise in each commodity separately, using a
price elasticity of supply of 1.0; and a one per
cent rise in all commodities together, where the
own price elasticity of supply is adjusted to
account for the fact that cross elasticities are not
included. The results are shown in Table 4.7.
     The main conclusions are that Germany can expect
to gain its largest transfer (arising from common
financing and community preference) through an increase in butter prices, which for the United
Kingdom would involve the largest losses. Also, he
shows that Italy's continued argument for special
treatment of imports of beef and veal is justified
from a national cost standpoint. France would be
the outstanding beneficiary of a price increase in
any product.

Tangermann[11]   Professor S. Tangermann of the
University of Gottingen, in the appendix to a study
assessing Germany's role within the CAP. presents
some results analysing the effects of abolishing
MCAs. Tangermann's model is similar in concept to
that of the IFS. It includes grain, sugar, beef
and veal, pork, poultry, eggs and milk. The elasticities used are 0.7 for supply and -0.2 for demand.
Perhaps the largest difference in treatment is that
prices are not used directly, but are computed as
monetary unit values of supply and demand.

Table 4.7 : National Net Transfer Payments with Respect to a One Per Cent Common Price Increase Due to the Common Market Organisation : Koester.

(1975, million ua)

Country	Soft Wheat	Barley	White Sugar	Beef & Veal	Butter	Skim Milk Powder
(Elasticity of supply = 1)						
F.R. Germany	-1.218	-1.415	609	-2.715	2.517	1.372
France	9.221	3.231	-669	2.708	2.141	1.711
Italy	-1.386	-815	550	-7.510	-2.811	-2.782
Netherlands	-950	-147	-581	979	3.407	-101
United Kingdom	-4.689	-457	-329	-3.479	-8.847	-1.544
(Elasticity of supply = 0.3)						
F.R. Germany	-1.318	-1.519	0.788	-1.648	1.879	1.285
France	9.462	3.297	2.390	2.493	1.278	1.423
Italy	-1.380	-1.094	-0.611	-7.288	-1.318	-2.445
Netherlands	-1.002	-0.240	0.229	0.911	2.641	-0.185
United Kingdom	-4.751	-0.323	-3.373	-3.293	-6.813	-1.242

SOURCE : Koester, U. "The Redistributional Effects of the Common Agricultural Financial System". European Review of Agricultural Economics, 4, (4) pp. 321-325.

In Table 4.8 Tangermann's estimates of the abolition of MCAs are compared with those of the CEPG. The results should be comparable given that they apply to the same time period. However, the only reasonable similarities between these two sets of figures are that the United Kingdom and Netherlands can be expected to be net losers from the change, and Ireland is expected to be a net gainer.

Table 4.8 : Effects of Abolishing MCAs

		(1979, £ million)
Country	CEPG	Tangermann[a]
Germany	+16	-88
France	+231	-23
Italy	-34	-283
Belgium/Luxembourg	-1	-25
Netherlands	-76	-41
United Kingdom	-207	-365
Ireland	+25	+87
Denmark	-68	-

a. Converted from EUAs to £s at the rate
    of 0.664.

SOURCE : Cambridge Economic Policy Group.
         "Policies of the EEC". Chapter 2, in
         Cambridge Economic Policy Review, Vol.5,
         Gower Press, Cambridge.

         Tangermann, S. (1979) "Germany's Role
         within the CAP : Domestic Problems in
         International Perspective". Journal
         of Agricultural Economics. 30(3),
         pp. 241-260.

Tangermann also provides estimates of the effects of a one per cent devaluation of the green pound. The resultant cost to the United Kingdom of about £15 million compares reasonably with Morris' figure of about £21.5 million, given that Morris includes more commodities.

Schmitz[12] The study by Schmitz contains an analysis of the effect on Germany, France and the United Kingdom of price harmonisation at the common EC price level in 1976. Because different MCAs were applied, this study is not directly comparable with that of Tangermann or the CEPG. The modelling framework in which the analysis is completed is similar to that of Rollo and Warwick in that a reference situation of national financing at the same price level is used. The model incorporates the seven commodities: soft wheat, barley, white sugar, butter, beef, pork and skim milk powder. Schmitz uses demand elasticities between -0.15 and -0.6 and supply elasticities of 0.3 or 0.4. The net gains from harmonisation over these seven commodities for Germany are about -367 million EUA, for France about +241 million EUA and for the United Kingdom about -196 million EUA.

Von Witzke[13] In contrast to the previous studies, which attempt to measure the effects of price changes in CAP in terms of inter-country transfers, Von Witzke assesses the distributional effects within a single country. Using Lorenz curve and Gini coefficient analysis, the short- and long-run income distributional effects of continued upward movement in CAP prices in the Lower Saxony region of Germany are measured.
    The results of the analysis indicate that in the short-run (less than one year) the general effect of price increases is to decrease the concentration of agricultural income. In the long run (eight to ten years) the opposite result was observed. Von Witzke concludes that because of such long-run adverse effects on the income distribution the CAP should be replaced by some other income-supporting policy.

Ritson and Tangermann[14] In their economic and political analysis of the MCA system, Ritson and Tangermann suggest that the MCA system may be flexible enough to allow member countries to move towards their individual domestic agricultural policy objectives. A country would be expected to desire higher agricultural prices if it is a net exporter, has a poor farm structure, and/or has a high average non-farm income level. A country-by-country appraisal reveals that these conditions are more prevalent in high positive MCA countries than in countries which have negative MCAs. For example, Germany has the highest prices and also a poor farm structure and high non-farm incomes, but the fact that it is a net agricultural importer may diminish

the drive for even higher prices. In contrast, the
United Kingdom has had the lowest prices, and is a
net agricultural importer with a good farm structure,
and relatively low non-agricultural incomes. Hence,
the evidence supported their hypothesis up to 1978,
however the British policy for green rates since
1978 appears to require a different explanation.
The second part of their study is a geometric analysis of the MCA system into which has been built the
terms of trade effect of EC exports to the rest of
the world. The framework of the current study,
Chapter 3, builds on this work.

STUDIES OF THE MACROECONOMIC EFFECTS OF
GREEN POUND CHANGES

Dickinson and Wildgoose[15] and Dickinson et al[16] of
MAFF, and Rickard[17] of the British National Farmers'
Union, tackle the problem of defining a framework in
which to assess the wider effects of a green pound
devaluation on gross domestic product (GDP) in the
United Kingdom. The preliminary results contained
in these papers show the outcome to be highly sensitive to input assumptions, particularly demand and
supply elasticities, but they indicate the effects
of a green pound devaluation on real GDP in the
United Kingdom to be positive.

SUMMARY OF RECENT PAPERS APPRAISING
CHANGES IN THE CAP

The papers considered here are mainly concerned with
the inter-country transfers which occur as a result
of common price increases and changes in the level
of MCAs. The studies use a broadly similar analytical framework, but because they use different,
though reasonable, data bases, the overall results
differ. About the only common item in these results
is that the United Kingdom is expected to lose from
both common price increases and abolition of MCAs.
Little comparison is possible between the studies
evaluating MCA changes because they are based on
different time periods when different MCAs were
applicable. The principal studies considering price
changes are those of the IFS and Koester. The
following figures again reveal the difficulty of
comparison. Using a model with 17 commodities, the
IFS estimates the loss to the United Kingdom in 1978
of a one per cent price increase in all commodities
to be £21.9 million. Koester with his six commodity
1975 model estimates the loss to be £8.3 million.
The problem is that it is difficult to decide

whether it is the difference in time period or
commodity coverage or both that causes estimates of
the loss to differ.

CONCLUSIONS ON PREVIOUS STUDIES

In short there is now a considerable literature containing empirical and qualitative analysis of one
measure of the cost of the CAP (namely the budget
and trade effect), and much evidence of this effect
on the member countries of some marginal changes in
CAP. On both of these points there are wide discrepancies in the magnitude, and sometimes even the
sign, of the effects on member countries. It has
not been possible to pinpoint the source of these
discrepancies but it seems that apart from data
problems, there is substantial room for variation in
the definition of the concepts of cost used and the
specification of the alternative policy analysed.

NOTES

1. Blancus, P. (1978). "The Common Agricultural
Policy and the Balance of Payments of the EEC Member
Countries". Quarterly Review of Banca Naxionale del
Lavoro. 5,(3). pp.355-70.

2. Morris, C.N. (1980). "The Common Agricultural
Policy". Fiscal Studies 1,(2) pp.17-35. "The
Common Agricultural Policy : Sources and Methods".
IFS Working Paper No. 6. Institute for Fiscal
Studies, London.

3. Morris, C.N. IFS Working Paper (op. cit.).
pp. 28-30.

4. Bacon, R., Godley, W. and McFarquhar, A. (1978).
"The Direct Cost to Britain of Belonging to the EEC"
Chapter 5 in Cambridge Economic Policy Review, Vol.
4, Gower Press, Cambridge.

Cambridge Economic Policy Group (1979). "Policies
of the EEC". Chapter 2, in Cambridge Economic
Policy Review, Vol. 5, Gower Press, Cambridge.

McFarquhar, A., Godley, W. and Silvey, D. (1977).
"The Cost of Food and Britain's Membership of the
EEC". Chapter 3 in Cambridge Economic Policy Review
Gower Press, Cambridge.

5. Rollo, J.N.C. and Warwick, K.S. (1979). "The
CAP and Resource Flows among EEC Member States".

Government Economic Service Working Paper No. 27.
Ministry of Agriculture, Fisheries and Food. London.

6. Koester, U. (1977). "The Redistributional
Effects of the Common Agricultural Financial System"
European Review of Agricultural Economics. 4, (4)
pp.321-345.

7. Blancus, op. cit.

8. Morris, op. cit.

9. Cambridge Economic Policy Group, op. cit.

10. Koester, (op. cit.) concentrates on the effects
of price changes.

11. Tangermann, op. cit.

12. Schmitz, P.N. (1979). "EC Price Harmonisation:
A Macroeconomic Approach". European Review of
Agricultural Economics. 6, (2) pp.165-90.

13. Von Witzke, H. (1979). "Prices, Common Agri-
cultural Price Policy and Personal Distribution of
Incomes in West German Agriculture". European
Review of Agricultural Economics. 6, (1) pp.61-80.

14. Ritson, C. and Tangermann, S. (1979). "The
Economics and Politics of Monetary Compensatory
Amounts". European Review of Agricultural Economics
6, (2) pp.119-64.

15. Dickinson, S. and Wildgoose, J. (1979). "A
Framework for Assessing the Economic Effects of a
Green Pound Devaluation". Government Economic
Service Working Paper No. 23. Ministry of Agricul-
ture, Fisheries and Food, London.

16. Dickinson, S. et al (1980). "Effects of a
Green Pound Devaluation". Paper presented at the
Centre for European Agricultural Studies Workshop,
Wye College, Ashford. February.

17. Gawith, A. and Rickard, S. (1980). "The
Economic Effects of a Green Pound Devaluation".
Paper presented at the Centre for European Agricul-
tural Studies Workshop, Wye College, Ashford.
February.

Chapter 5

A MARKET/BUDGET MODEL OF THE CAP

INTRODUCTION

The previous chapters have described the background
to the present attempt at costing the CAP, including
the theoretical framework of economic analysis used.
This and the following chapters report the results
of calculations of the market and budgetary effects
of both the present Common Agricultural Policy and
some alternative policies. In the present chapter,
the broad nature of these calculations are described
in a non-mathematical way, and the scope and coverage of the analysis are explained by description and
the presentation of some numerical results. Chapter
6 outlines the policy alternatives included in the
present study, with their analytical and institutional implications, and discusses the results at a
high level of aggregation. Chapters 7 and 8 discuss
the results at more detailed levels by commodity and
country.
        The calculations were obtained by writing and
running a computer programme[1] to simulate the
physical and financial flows occurring under a
'base' policy corresponding to the CAP in 1980 -
'CAP 1980' - and those which might occur under four
specified alternative policies. The use of such a
model permits a large number of computations to be
carried out and revised, at a level of detail quite
impracticable with any other method. Simulation
results are therefore available in great volume, but
only the most important figures are discussed in
this chapter.
        The economic model used is composed of a set of
conventional, partial equilibrium, supply-and-demand
models (as outlined in Chapter 3) for each of the sixteen agricultural commodities in each of the eight
member states of the Community (Luxembourg being
included with Belgium throughout). Given a set of

69

prices and other policy parameters such as quota levels, such models can be solved for the quantities of production, consumption and trade in each member state. The expenditure corresponding to the support arrangements as applied to these physical flows can then be calculated. Alternatively, given conditions on quantities (such as a given degree of self-supply or a desired balance of trade) the corresponding prices necessary to achieve these conditions can be estimated. Comparison of the results for CAP 1980 and alternative situations will indicate the relative costs and benefits that accrue in various ways from different courses of policy action. Each of the following sections describes a facet of this framework of calculations.

POLICY INSTRUMENTS

The policy instruments represented in the model include the major expenditure categories of the Guarantee Section of the European Agricultural Guidance and Guarantee Fund (FEOGA). These are (a) intervention in the internal markets of the Community, both by subsidies and aid to private-sector production, handling, storage and disposal of agricultural products, and the market-supporting activities of the intervention agencies, (b) refunds on agricultural exports to non-member countries, and agricultural levies on imports, and (c) monetary compensatory amounts (MCAs). Each of these expenditures is governed mainly by the price and subsidy levels set at intervals by the Council of Ministers. In addition, there are certain other policy instruments for specific commodities, for example, production quotas for sugar and import agreements for beef, which may involve flows into, and out of, the Community budget.
    Changes in the CAP are simulated in the model by alteration in the levels of these instruments. The corresponding impacts on the various quantity and expenditure levels are taken to represent the effect of the corresponding policy changes. However, from the description of the EC and the CAP in Chapter 2, it will be recognised that these calculations omit some of the elements in the full programme of activities of the Policy. For example, certain agricultural expenditures such as those on food aid and structural guidance are not included in the present study. Moreover, the financing of the overall Community budget is taken to remain substantially as at present. Attention is thus focussed on the implications of altering the agricultural price

policies of the CAP for the FEOGA section of the budget, and on the economic effects of such alterations for producers, consumers and traders of agricultural products.

COMMODITIES

The model includes 16 commodities which in 1979 accounted for about two thirds of final agricultural production in the Community and three quarters of FEOGA expenditure (excluding transitional accessionary expenditure and MCAs). The commodities are as follows: Crops: common wheat, durum wheat, barley, oats, rye and meslin, maize and sugar beet. Livestock products: pigmeat, poultrymeat, eggs, beef and veal, butter, cheese, skimmed milk powder, cream and condensed milk. The major CAP commodities excluded are rice, tobacco, olive oil, wine, fruit and vegetables, and sheepmeat, most of which are specialist products confined to specific regions in the Community. Potatoes are omitted as this product is not yet incorporated into the common market organisation. Liquid milk has also been excluded, in favour of the five listed manufactured dairy products, to which the policy instruments of CAP analysed here apply in practice. The exclusion of those commodities will result in under-estimation of the budgetary and economic consequences of the modelled policy changes to the extent that these changes are envisaged as applying to commodities other than the sixteen above. It can be argued that some at least of the excluded commodities would be likely to be treated seperately from general changes to the CAP of the type modelled in the present study, and hence the above biases are likely to be less serious than at first appears.

For each of the included commodities, and each of the member states, data was assembled for 1977 (crops 1977/78), and updated to 1980 (1980/81). The set of earlier data provides a base on which direct comparison of actual and simulated budgetary flows can be carried out. The updated data-base is the starting-point from which alternative policy situations are calculated. Data for the following variables were required as base-level input:

domestic production and utilisation (including seed and animal feed);

imports to and exports from third countries, administered and world prices; and

subsidy rates per tonne on production,
consumption and for private storage, and
total expenditure on public storage.

Production and utilisation figures were taken
from published data[2] for 1977 and include changes in
stocks. The 1980 estimates are based on supply and
demand growth rates modified by technical economic,
and demographic factors, with stock changes set at
zero to simulate a no-change situation. Import and
export volumes and subsidy levels were initially set
at their published levels for 1977, and modified by
inflationary and trade changes for 1980. The administered prices used were those guaranteed by the
intervention agencies of the Community (the intervention prices). For pigmeat, the basic price was
used, and for eggs and poultrymeat, minimum import
(sluice gate) prices were employed. Certain world
prices were taken as unit-values, published for 1977
and estimated for 1980.

SUPPLY AND DEMAND CALCULATIONS

In order to run the model for any specified policy
(e.g. alteration of support prices, or free trade),
prices are either set or calculated in each country
for each commodity. Where new prices are set under
an alternative policy, the calculation of the
corresponding supply and demand quantities, and the
trade and budgetary consequences which flow from
these, are performed in a manner to be described
below. However, other policies are defined in terms
of desired quantitative or market conditions (e.g.
equilibrium free trade) whose pricing implications
must themselves be calculated. Given the interrelationships between products, this is a complex
task, and the adopted procedure repeats the calculations several times with varying sets of prices until a mutually consistent set of commodity prices is
obtained which achieves the specified quantitative
or market conditions of the policy. As far as is
known from theoretical considerations and in practice, such a solution is unique.

Given the base data described in the previous
section, the calculations of supply and demand responses to changes in administered prices, and those
of the prices necessary to achieve policy aims in
quantity terms, employ the economic concept of elasticity - the percentage change in quantity supplied
or demanded for a one per cent change in price. Own-
price elasticities refer to the effect of a change
in the price of a product on the quantity supplied
or demanded of the same product; cross-price

72

elasticities relate a price change to the effect on the quantity of another product. The latter are important in cases where one commodity is used as an input to the production of another (e.g. cereals for meat) or where substitution between products is possible, either in production (e.g. crops and grazing livestock) or consumption (e.g. beef and pigmeat).

For the present study lack of resources, and some a priori judgement of the marginal costs and benefits of research effort precluded the full specification, estimation and testing of an integrated set of structural supply and demand equations for all CAP commodities for each member state. As a substitute, supply and demand elasticity matrices for the major commodities have been developed as a set of "experimental values" currently applied uniformly for each member country. These are given in Table 5.1. In choosing these values, published research has been taken into account. The values used here are intended to reflect long run, full adjustment responses, as required for comparative-static analysis. As experimental values, the intention is to subject them to change and sensitivity analysis, not to regard them as ex-cathedra statements.

Within the commodity groups given, barley and butter are taken as the representative products for supply response to cross-price changes, while the supply response shown for cereals with respect to cereal prices reflects intra-cereal competition for resources explicitly recognised in the full specification of the matrix, grain by grain. On the demand side, the effect on cereal feed demand of changes in livestock prices is related to the own-price supply elasticities of the livestock products and to the utilization of cereals (taken as barley and maize) by livestock groups. Using the elasticities in Table 5.1, each country's gross surplus or deficit position is determined using constant-elasticity (log-linear) supply and demand curves calibrated to the base-data price and quantity levels.

The next step in the model calculations is to estimate how these gross surpluses are disposed of, and deficits satisfied. After any adjustment required for changes in stocks and for net third-country trade positions, the resulting net surpluses and deficits in each country are available, from which extra- and intra-community trade flows remain to be calculated. With regard to extra-community flows, the exportable surplus, or import requirement, of the Community as a whole influences world prices alongside the surpluses and deficits of all other

Table 5.1 : Model Supply and Demand Elasticities

| | Change in Quantity Supplied of: | | | | |
	Cereals	Pigmeat	Poultry	Beef	Milk
Price change in:					
Cereals	+0.4	-0.75	-0.75	-0.2	-0.5
Pigmeat	0	+1.0	-0.2	0	0
Poultry	0	-0.2	+1.0	0	0
Beef	0	0	0	+1.0	+0.1
Milk	-0.3	0	0	+0.5	+1.0
	Change in quantity Demanded of:				
	Cereals	Pigmeat	Poultry	Beef	Milk
Price change in:					
Cereals	-0.5	0	0	0	0
Pigmeat	+0.15	-0.5	0	+0.2	0
Poultry	+0.15	0	-0.5	+0.05	0
Beef	+0.05	+0.3	+0.15	-0.5	0
Milk	+0.13	0	0	0	-0.5

NOTE: Rest-of-the-world supply and demand elasticities with respect to world prices were taken
as follows: cereals, beef and veal, 1.0 and
-0.5 respectively; sugar 1.5 and -0.1; pigmeat 0.6 and -0.3; poultry and eggs 0.6 and
-0.2; milk products 0.3 and -0.1. The choice
of these values is intended to reflect the
degree to which these products are insulated
from world trading prices by domestic policies in the rest of the world.

trading countries. In the model, these world prices
are determined by the interaction between the overall EC surplus/deficit schedule and that of non-EC
countries. Points on the latter curve are generated
by the 'rest-of-the-world' supply and demand elasticities specified in the footnote to Table 5.1,
calibrated to the base levels of world market price
and the total world production of each commodity.
The procedure is equivalent to constructing the
'excess' supply/demand schedules for the EC and the
rest of the world, and finding the point of balance
between these two complements of the world market,

each under their separate pricing and supply conditions.

For intra-Community trade, since import levies and export refunds bring world prices to Community levels, and MCAs compensate EC traders for inter-member price differentials, there are no economic price signals (at least at this level of simplification) on which trade flows can be presumed to depend. Hence the following procedure has been adopted. The separate sums of the net surpluses and deficits defined above are compared to determine whether the Community is in overall surplus or deficit after allowing for 'normal' stock changes and third-country trade flows. If the EC is in surplus, deficit countries are supplied from the other countries in proportion to their surpluses (with the exception that a UK deficit is first supplied with any surplus from Eire). Remaining surpluses are exported to third countries, thus increasing some members' net exports above base level. If the Community as a whole is in deficit, any available surpluses are similarly distributed and the remainder is imported from the rest of the world. The results of this somewhat arbitrary procedure are to ensure that trade flows take place between most member countries at levels which are not too different from those currently observed, but so as to reflect trade changes in expected directions. Apart from the theoretical difficulty mentioned above, consistent data on intra-Community trade are not available on which to build or calibrate any detailed alternative procedure.

BUDGETARY CALCULATIONS

Each of the main budgetary flows taking place under the Guarantee section of FEOGA as a result of the agricultural support policies of the Community are calculated for each commodity and member state. Expenditures - export refunds, intervention payments and MCAs - represent transfers from the Community exchequer to the recipient nation, while agricultural import levies and sugar levies constitute revenue sources also arising directly out of the operation of agricultural policy. Receipts from the common external tariff on non-agricultural goods and from each member's direct VAT or GNP contributions fund the net agricultural deficit (for 1980 this takes into account the revised financial mechanism agreed in that year). Changes in policy are reflected in changes in these flows according to the impact made on production, consumption and trading levels, and on price differentials. The various policy alternatives therefore have complex consequences for the pattern of public-finance flows between both member-states and commodities.

Export refunds are calculated within the model for each country and commodity as the product of exports to third countries and the difference between the world and intervention prices. Import levies are calculated on the product of third country imports and the same price differential, modified to take account of various institutional complications and trade agreements. These include MCAs additional to, or offsetting, refund and levy payments, the retention of a ten per cent administrative charge by the levy-collecting agencies, and various commodity agreements on beef, butter and sugar. Of the various forms of intervention undertaken by the Community, subsidies on cereals, sugar and certain milk products are estimated by applying a rate per tonne calculated from the published totals actually spent in each country to the base levels of each commodity. Aids to private storage of sugar, pigmeat, beef and veal, and butter are similarly estimated in proportion to production. Storage by the authorities themselves are entered as total expenditure amounts. The use of these calculations thus assumes that the Community will adopt similar policies and costs with regard to storage under alternative price policies. MCAs, being border taxes and subsidies applied to allow national price differentials to exist, are ascribed to the member-state importing or exporting the product in question. (In practice, actual MCAs are not all applied in this way, and the recorded budgetary flows reflect the various modifications made by the Community in order to minimise budgetary expenditure, as noted in Chapter 3. Such complications were considered negligible for the model calculations.) Finally, production levies on any "B-quota' sugar produced in each member state are computed.

In Community budgetary practice, as in most sets of accounts, the principles of unity and universality[3] are in general followed, in that income from all sources is tabulated separately from expenditure. However, for the present purposes, a separate FEOGA guarantee section budget is required in order to isolate and study the financial impact of changes in the CAP. Hence the budgetary items above are computed within the model for each commodity and country under a given policy, and compiled in the following manner:

Table 5.2 : Model Format of FEOGA Budget

Expenditure	Income
Export refunds	Import levies
Intervention payments	Sugar levies
MCAs	
Other expenditure items	
Gross expenditure	minus Gross Income
Net FEOGA Expenditure	

A similar set of accounts is in practice published by the Commission as part of the background
information accompanying their preliminary draft
budgets each year.[4] It should be noted that, partly
as a consequence of the exclusion of liquid milk
from model coverage, co-responsibility levy revenues
on milk do not appear in the Table 5.2.

NON-BUDGETARY CALCULATIONS

Having determined the quantities of each commodity
produced, consumed and stored within each member
state, and the trade flows with each other member
and with the rest of the world as a whole, for the
base situation and for alternative policies, the
calculation of various economic magnitudes is com-
paratively straightforward.

The self-supply ratio, defined as the utilisation of a commodity expressed as a percentage of
production, is an indicator of the extent to which
individual countries and the Community itself are
likely to be sensitive to changes in trade policy
or conditions. Valuing production and consumption
at producer and consumer prices respectively, it is
also possible to calculate overall self-supply
ratios for each country and for the Community.
Table 5.3 gives some values for the base 1980 position, as estimated from the model.

It will be noted that the Community is already in
considerable surplus in each commodity category,
especially milk products, which give the Netherlands, Eire and Denmark overall self-supply ratios
of over 200. Italy and the United Kingdom are the
only two countries still in significant deficit,
with West Germany almost exactly in balance, and

Table 5.3 : Self-Supply Ratios, 1980 Base Position.

Commodity Group	WG	F	I	NE	BE/L	UK	IR	DK	EC
Cereals	91	188	84	43	58	93	104	148	112
Sugar	129	210	114	158	205	47	131	167	128
Milk Products	141	147	87	407	104	84	730	452	151
Other Livestock Products	81	89	81	188	162	101	340	264	102
Overall	96	126	83	216	130	86	307	237	112

Notes : For explanation of 1980 base position, and coverage of table, see text.

SOURCE : Authors' estimates.

France, a large producer, in considerable surplus. It is of course the existence and balance of these surpluses and deficits, and their movements over time and in response to policy shifts, that underlie most of the debate over the development of the CAP.

A further non-budgetary consequence for a trading nation of a policy change is the effect on the balance of trade in the commodities involved. These have been calculated before the imposition of refunds on exports or levies on imports (including any MCAs) so as to arrive at a 'private sector' balance of agricultural trade reflecting the foreign exchange dealings of each country's importers and exporters. For third-country trade, imports and exports are therefore valued at world prices, while intra-member trade is assumed to take place at administered prices. Aside from MCA complications, the trade balances thus computed correspond to the entries in each nation's balance of payments accounts under the heading of imports and exports of goods and services. (See areas $X + Y + C_1 + E_1$ and $X + Y + C_1 + F_1$ in Figure 3.3).

Table 5.4 reports some results for the base 1980 position. The overall figures emphasise the profoundly different position of member-states even more than the self-supply ratios, since they reflect the impact of Community preference in agricultural trade. France, the Netherlands, Eire and Denmark are major foreign-exchange earners on this 'private sector' agricultural trade account, while West Germany, Italy and the United Kingdom show substantial deficits.

Further calculations produce the various national balances of trade and of payments which have been described in Chapter 3. Briefly, these comprise:

(i) The financial contribution paid by each member state towards the net cost of Community expenditure under the FEOGA guarantee and market organisation systems. This is calculated, for any particular policy, by allocating the total Community net cost according to the percentage share of total VAT contributions as occurs under the base policy, since it is these contributions which constitute the marginal component of CAP finances.

Table 5.4 : Balances of Trade, 1980 Base Position

(mEUA)

Commodity Group	WG	F	I	NE	BE/L	UK	IR	DK	EC
Cereals	-269	2478	-326	-172	-168	-205	3	386	1626
Sugar	203	693	59	106	142	-426	14	57	846
Milk Products	157	487	-533	1168	-228	-563	714	224	1427
Other Livestock Products	-1604	-892	-1149	1379	938	72	826	972	542
Total	-1513	2765	-1948	2481	684	-1123	1557	1538	4441

SOURCE : Authros' estimates.

(ii)   The <u>balance of FEOGA payments</u>, i.e.
the sum of (i) above and net FEOGA
expenditure in the member state
concerned. For the Community as a
whole, these balances cancel out,
but they may reach substantial
levels of 'official' flows across
the exchanges for individual countries.

(iii)   The overall <u>balance of agricultural
payments</u>, i.e. the sum of (ii)
above and the 'private' balance of
trade explained above. This represents the contribution (positive
or negative) to the national
balance of payments made by all
financial flows arising from agricultural trade and policy encom-
passed by the model.

(iv)   The <u>preferential trade effect</u> and
the <u>budget and trade effect</u> (see
Chapter 3) representing the net
benefit or cost of trading at
Community rather than world price
levels. Again, for the Community
as a whole, these effects cancel
out, since they represent equal
and opposite changes in trade and
budgetary flows.

Table 5.5 shows these various balances as calculated for the base-policy position in 1980.

A final group of non-budgetary calculations is
carried out to arrive at estimates of changes in the
economic welfare of taxpayers, producers and consumers as a result of a move from the base to an
alternative policy. The first of these is simply
the difference between the VAT-based contributions
made by each member state to finance the net FEOGA
expenditure of Table 5.2, under the two policies.
This implies that the changes in the financing requirements are reflected back to taxpayers through
adjustments in national fiscal policies, either
through direct changes in taxation or equivalent
changes in expenditures by national governments.
This in turn implies that the financial contributions by member states to the EC budget are 'additional' to their own national budgets.

Changes in producer and consumer welfare are
calculated for both groups as explained in Chapter 3,
for each commodity and in each country. These are
then aggregated to give overall producer and

Table 5.5 : Trade and Payments Balances, 1980 Base Position

(mEUA)

Item	WG	F	I	NE	BE/L	UK	IR	DK	EC9
Net FEOGA Expenditure	1820	2301	928	1300	206	-24	623	1097	8255
Financial Contribution	2707	2037	900	500	391	1433	71	217	8255
Balance of FEOGA Payments	-887	265	28	800	-185	-1457	552	880	0
Balance of Agricultural Trade	-1513	2765	-1948	2481	684	-1123	1557	1538	4441
Balance of Agricultural Payments	-2400	3030	-1920	3281	499	-2579	2109	2418	4441
Preferential Trade Effect	-853	-301	-961	1146	333	-465	604	497	0
Budget and Trade Effect	-1740	-36	-933	1946	+148	-1922	+1156	+1377	0

Note : For item definitions, see text.
SOURCE : Authors' estimates.

and consumer welfare changes. However, account must
be taken of the important proportion of cereals produced in the EC and utilised as livestock feed, since
rises in cereal prices clearly benefits some farmers
but penalises others. The procedure adopted is to
reduce the gross effects on producer and consumer
economic welfare in each country by the estimated
change in the value of feed cereals. As a cost, this
change in value affects the position of livestock
farmers, but does not affect consumers beyond the
farmgate except through higher livestock product
prices. For each of the main livestock categories -
pigmeat, poultrymeat, eggs, dairy and beef - technical coefficients are used to relate changes in production levels to changes in feed usages and values. The
surplus measures for each category of livestock producer, and for cereal producers as a whole, are then
adjusted accordingly. This procedure is admittedly
crude but takes some account of this important relationship internal to the farming sector. Other possible amendments to the producer and consumer economic
welfare measures such as factor cost effects, and
real-income compensations for food price changes,
have not been allowed for since they involve consideration beyond the scope of this study. The numerical results of the producer, consumer and taxpayer
welfare calculations are deferred until specific alternative policies are discussed in Chapter 6.

BASE POLICY RESULTS

As an illustration of the budgetary magnitudes involved, and as a form of model validation, Table 5.6
gives some Community-level results for the two base
years used in the present study, 1977 and 1980,
along with published Commission figures, insofar as
these can be reconciled with the model categories.
Items which fall outside the modelled system include accessionary compensatory amounts (ACAs), which
in 1977 were still payable to the 1973 entrants but
were being phased out, co-responsibility levies on
milk, and subsidies on food aid. The 1977 columns
indicate quite a good fit, although more detailed
comparison shows some over-estimation of sugar
export refund expenditure, compensated by under-
estimation of expenditure on milk. This is under-
standable when one considers the intermittent nature
of the EC export tendering system, and the carry-
over of stocks from previous years. It will be
noted that in 1977, nearly 40 per cent of the gross
expenditure incurred under the CAP was offset by
receipts from agricultural sources.

Table 5.6 : The Community Agricultural Budget:
Comparison of Actual with Model
Results, 1977 and 1980 Base Positions.

Item	1977 actual	1977 model	1980 EC	1980 model
	mEUAs		mEUAs	
Export Refunds	2087	1924	4824	6161
Intervention:				
- Producer Subsidies		229		256
- Consumer Subsidies		604		226
- Private Storage		272		300
- Public Storage		633		620
- Total	2046	1738	3790	1402
MCAs	860	404	276	139
Other Expenditure	985	1606	2616	3564
Gross FEOGA Expenditure	5978	5673	11507	11267
Import Levies:				
- Included		1088		1992
- Excluded		799		799
- Total	1817	1757	1719	2791
Sugar Levies	321	200	504	220
Gross FEOGA Income	2314	2087	2224	3012
Net FEOGA Expenditure	3664	3586	9283	8255

SOURCE : EC Commission, Agricultural Situation in
the Community, 1977 and 1980 reports,
and Authors' estimates.

The 1980 comparison is fairly satisfactory at
the aggregate level, but there is some over-
estimation of export refund expenditure, and of
import levy income. This is probably due mostly to
the use of inappropriate world prices - the Community
will naturally try to buy (import) when world prices
are low, and sell (export) when high - but part of
the discrepancy is due to under-estimation in the

figures produced by the Commission which had to bring
in supplementary budgets in 1980 to cope with unexpectedly large expenditures. Also, the violent monetary fluctuations of 1980 resulted in unanticipated
changes in budgetary flows, not captured by the
model. Nevertheless, despite incomplete coverage
and the simplicity of its calculations relative to
the complexities of the real world, the model appears
to simulate fairly successfully the actual FEOGA expenditures and receipts. This gives some confidence
that the results of running the model under alternative policy situations will not be seriously mis-
leading, and should help to clarify the issues
raised, if not to quantify exactly the changing magnitude of each budgetary item.

NOTES

1.   As with all large computer models (and economic data), the process of revision and development
in the hands of a research team appears endless.
This chapter describes the situation as of mid-
summer 1981.

2.   The main source of the original data was:
Commission of the European Communities, The Agricultural Situation in the Community : 1977 Report,
Brussels, 1978, updated by reference to later volumes. A useful supplement was found to be: Ministry
of Agriculture, Fisheries and Food, EEC Agricultural
and Food Statistics (1974-77), London, 1978.

3.   Strasser, D., The Finances of Europe,
Commission of the European Communities, Brussels,
1981, pp. 19-22.

4.   Op. cit., p.185.

Chapter 6

POLICY COMPARISONS

The present study takes an eclectic approach to the
comparison of agricultural policy options; several
alternative policies have been chosen to provide
market and budgetary positions which may be compared
with those at the base position of 'CAP 1980'. The
alternatives detailed below clearly do not exhaust
the possibilities, but they do range from marginal
adjustments in current policy parameters, to much
more drastic changes in the economic environment of
Community agriculture. In choosing the particular
alternative policies described below, it is not implied that any or all of them are to be preferred to
the current situation reflected by the base policy.
It will become clear that any alternative involves
deterioration in the economic position of at least
one set of consumers, producers or taxpayers, and an
overall judgement on a 'best' or at least 'better'
agricultural policy involves political judgements
which will not be discussed here. However, it is
recognised that a degree of professional judgement
has been brought to bear on the selection of the
alternative policies (as of the overall subject of
study), and the choices actually made may be justified on a variety of grounds, some oriented towards
the observed realities of policymaking, others towards simplicity of concepts and calculations.
Other policies will no doubt occur to the reader,
and it is part of the potential strength of the
modelling technique employed in the present study
that it should be possible to adapt the methodology
to a wide range of possible alternatives.
    In this chapter, four alternative policies are
described - the 1980 EC 'price package', harmonisation of Community prices, Community self-sufficiency,
and a free market in agricultural products - and
their effects at the level of the Community are
analysed and discussed. Chapters 7 and 8 discuss

the results at commodity and country level respectively, while Chapter 9 offers analyses of their distributional and efficiency implications.

THE 1980 PRICE PACKAGE

In April 1980, the Council of Ministers adopted a set of measures for the further development of the CAP which included nominal rises in support prices for agricultural products averaging about 4½ per cent. The package represented a compromise between the Commission proposals for a 2-2½ per cent average nominal rise and farmer-lobby pressure for a figure nearer 7 per cent.[1] Although Ministers were criticised, and perhaps rightly, for approving price rises even for products in persistent surplus, the changes, when deflated for each country, represented a fall in real terms for many agricultural support prices (see Table 6.1).

Table 6.1 : 1980 CAP Price Changes.

Commodity	Change Price %	Country	1980 GNP/GDP Deflator
Cereals[1]	4.5	Germany	4.50
Sugar	5.3	France	10.75
Meats	4.0	Italy	18.00
Milk Products[2]	2.3	Netherlands	5.25
		Belgium/Luxembourg	5.00
Average	4.5	United Kingdom	19.00
		Eire	17.50
		Denmark	9.00

1. Except rye and meslin, 2.5 per cent.

2. Except cheese, 3.9 per cent, and skimmed milk powder (SMP), 4.9 per cent.

SOURCE : See Note 1, and Economic Outlook, Organisation for Economic Co-operation and Development, July 1980, Vol. 27.

The package in fact constituted the second major step in the policy of 'prudent' pricing first adopted by the Community in 1979/80 when the budgetary dangers that lay ahead became increasingly apparent. In Spring 1981, a third step in the same direction was avoided when unexpectedly high world prices relaxed the budgetary constraint, and the drop in Community farmers' real incomes during 1980/81 led to pressure being placed on achieving price rises at least roughly in line with inflation. However, the longer-term external forces are such that the cost-price squeeze can hardly be completely relaxed in anything but the short term, and the 1980 package seems likely to represent a more typical set of price changes than those of 1981.

In any event, an analysis of the equilibrium impact of these price changes on the Community's agriculture and finances is of interest as measuring, albeit in a long-run sense (see page 41), the effect of an actual policy decision. It is not so clear, however, what the 'alternative' to this policy should be. The base 'CAP 1980' policy itself incorporates the price levels agreed upon in April 1980, and hence it makes little sense to raise these price levels by a further amount, as though Ministers had agreed to double the percentage changes in the package. It seems more sensible to reduce the 1980 base price levels by these changes, so as to simulate the position as though no agreement had been reached, and the previous year's prices had continued to rule (in nominal terms). This also avoids the necessity to deflate the nominal price changes, since both the base and alternative policies are seen as affecting the year 1980 (ignoring, as elsewhere, inflationary trends within any one year).

The results of this procedure are reported in column (2) of Table 6.2, which should therefore be interpreted as the effect of not having reached agreement on the 1980 price package, and which should be compared with column (1) representing the base CAP 1980 position with the package in operation, or at least fully known. The main points of interest, are that, without the package:

(i) Community self-supply in agricultural products falls from 112 to 103, which represents a shift towards the elimination of surpluses.

(ii) Average real support prices fall by over four per cent, with consequential producer losses and 'consumer' gains of over 2500 million EUA.

Table 6.2 : Policy Comparisons at EC Level.

Item	1980 Base Position (1)	1980 Price Package (2)	Price Harmonisation (3)	Community Self-Sufficiency (4)	Free Market (5)
Self-supply (index)	112	108	110	100	82
Average real price change (%)	0.0	-4.3	-2.9	-13.5	-31.9
Budgetary Flows (mEUA):					
Export refunds	6161	5143	5748	1485	0
Intervention	1402	1381	1373	1249	0
MCAs (net)	139	111	0	-162	0
Excluded products	3565	3034	3350	1547	0
Gross FEOGA expenditure	11267	9669	10471	4119	0
FEOGA income	3012	3614	3458	1516	0
Net FEOGA expenditure	8255	6055	7012	2603	0
Balance of Trade (mEUA)	4441	3339	3669	372	-9041
Welfare Effects (mEUA):					
Producer	0	-2879	-2102	-9725	-22039
Consumer	0	2573	2266	7231	24836
Taxpayers	0	2220	1243	5652	8255
Overall	0	1894	1407	3158	11051

SOURCE : Authors' estimates.

90

(iii)   Net agricultural expenditure falls by
        a quarter from 8250 million EUA to
        6000 million EUA, due partly to a
        drop in expenditure and partly to a
        rise in levy income.

(iv)   Taxpayers gain by 1000 million EUA
        in comparison with the base position,
        leading to an overall net gain of
        economic welfare of about half this
        amount.

It could be concluded that the 1980 package as
finally agreed, although representing a fairly
rigorous attitude taken by the Council of Ministers
to the rising cost of CAP surpluses, by no means reversed the protective bias of the CAP towards agriculture (since the above effects were all avoided),
and denied to taxpayers and the general economy the
gains in (iv) above. On the other hand, the sharp
falls in Community self-supply, real support price
levels, and comparable net Community expenditure
under the 'no package' situation all point to the
serious and significant effects which would have resulted had Ministers attempted to maintain the
status quo in nominal prices in 1980. Of course,
this modelled comparison of the long-run equilibrium
position resulting from the application of the 1980
price-change package with the 1980 base position
ignores other (non-price) decisions by Ministers,
and the observed impact of a year-on-year change in
product price levels will be confounded by other
factors such as rising costs and environmental conditions, and the degree of responsiveness in the
system to these. However, the abstraction has
isolated some important aspects of the 1980 situation which may have been obscured by rising price
and expenditure levels of the CAP and the relentless
trend of increased production arising from technological progress, both of which arise from factors
outside the price-fixing negotiations.

HARMONISATION AT COMMON PRICES

Ever since their introduction in 1969, monetary compensatory amounts (MCAs) have represented non-
attainment of the objective set by the Community of
gradual harmonisation in economic and monetary
policies, in that they have enabled countries to
enjoy somewhat different price levels for agricultural products despite the declaration of 'common'
prices in Brussels each year. Although it can be

argued that MCAs have enabled agricultural trade to continue in accordance with the Community's agricultural rules, the fact remains that the unity of the various product markets has been broken into seven partial markets with different prices, linked by the border taxes and subsidies represented by MCAs. The dismantling of the MCA system therefore represents one means of moving more closely to the basic principles of the Community, and suggestions to this effect have continued to emanate from the Commission.[2]

However, there has been considerable resistance by member states to the elimination of the artificial green rates of conversion which, in the presence of widely fluctuating market exchange rates, have given rise to MCAs up to forty per cent in magnitude. For a given country, green rates provide a stabilising element which insulates its farmers from short-run changes in their output prices resulting from external factors affecting market exchange rates. The introduction of the European Monetary System (EMS) has somewhat reduced the importance of this argument, but MCAs remain useful for members not yet full participants in the EMS, namely the United Kingdom, whose currency is not explicitly stabilised through the EMS, and they continue to provide a buffer mechanism for other members in the event of an alteration in their EMS central rate. For Germany, in particular, positive MCAs maintain relatively high prices for the farmers, and provide some consolation for the high share of Community expenditure which that country has to finance.

In the middle-to-late 1970s, the average MCA was negative, indicating a preponderance of over-valued green currencies relative to 'common' prices expressed in EUAs and linked to the appreciating currencies of the former 'snake'. Thus harmonisation to common prices would have represented an overall raising of farm prices; and this has undoubtedly hardened the opposition to harmonisation proposals from member-states with lower-than-average price levels (negative MCAs). On the other hand, countries with relatively high prices would not have relished the necessary price reductions, let alone the additional contributions they would have had to make to the overall EC budget. More recent exchange-rate movements have diminished the MCA range (see Table 6.3). It should be noted, however, that in 1981, the combination of the EMS and MCA systems resulted in an unparallelled opportunity for many countries to achieve high national price increases despite relatively low rises in common price levels. This was possible through revaluations of the lire

and sterling within the EMS which created positive
MCA gaps between the green and market exchange rates
of most currencies. The 1981 package enabled these
gaps to be reduced resulting in a double boost to
nominal price levels in most member states.

Table 6.3 : Green Rates and MCA Percentages,
June 1980

Country	Green Rate (national currency/EUA)		MCA Percentage
West Germany	2.78	DM	+9.8
France	5.77	FF	0.0
Italy	1117	L	0.0
Netherlands	2.8	Fl	+1.8
Belgium/Luxembourg	40.6	BF	+1.8
United Kingdom	0.62	£	+3.32
Eire	0.60	£I	-1.35
Denmark	7.72	Kr	0.0

SOURCE : CAP Monitor, Agra-Europe (London) Ltd.

Ignoring such essentially short-run phenomena
the goal of price harmonisation remains an important
component of the Community's striving for market
unity. Consequently, one policy alternative which
is compared in this study with the base position is
harmonisation of national prices at the Community's
EUA support prices, for all CAP products. This is
equivalent to the elimination of the MCA arrangements and represents a policy shift in the direction
of further integration of the agricultural markets
of the Community.

The budgetary effect of such a policy shift will
include the elimination of MCA payments and receipts,
and changes in export refund expenditure and import
levy income. The magnitude of these changes will
depend on:

- relative changes in national prices
  consequent on price harmonisation;
- changes in quantities traded with the
  rest of the world as domestic production
  and consumption levels alter;
- changes in world price levels resulting
  from these trade alterations (the 'terms
  of trade' effect).

Columns (1) and (3) of Table 6.2 contain the major Community-level results for the 1980 base position and the harmonisation alternative outlined above. The major points of interest are that:

(i) Average Community self-supply alters only slightly, remaining well above 100.

(ii) Average prices fall by about three per cent (implying that the mid-1980 green currency structure tended to raise average Community farm prices above the 'common' level).

(iii) Net budgetary expenditure falls slightly, partly as a result of lower export refunds, i.e. costs of surplus disposal, and partly due to slightly higher income receipts.

(iv) MCAs are, of course, eliminated.

(v) Due to patterns of national self-sufficiency rates and MCA levels, the net sum of producer and consumer welfare measures show a slight gain, but taxpayers enjoy considerable relief leading to an overall welfare gain of 1400 million EUA for the Community as a whole.

Given the base position in 1980, when market exchange rates had restored average Community price levels to a position only slightly above those of common prices, it is a little surprising that the overall effect of harmonisation at Community level is by no means negligible. However, as (v) above indicates, this finding disguises important inter-country and inter-commodity effects, which are discussed more fully in Chapters 7 and 8.

COMMUNITY SELF-SUFFICIENCY

One of the declared objectives of the CAP is the guarantee of regular supplies of food. While this is not economically equivalent to the attaining of 100 per cent self-supply (self-sufficiency) in each agricultural commodity,3 expansion in those commodities for which Community consumption exceeds production is often urged for a variety of reasons. Higher levels of self-supply would insulate the Community further from the vicissitudes of a world market which may already be unstable even with the

94

EC as a significant importer. In certain countries, the balance of payments may be a source of macro-economic concern, and any measures reducing imports will possess appeal. Throughout the Community, higher self-supply is a convenient vehicle for farmer and landowner interests to raise the status of their interests.

From the opposite point of view, 100 per cent self-supply provides an equally convenient (if arbitrary) goal for those concerned with embarrassing surpluses of certain products, even though a small level of over-supply may in practice be desirable if other sources are unreliable. The semi-permanent structural agricultural surpluses that now threaten the Community, even in cereals, seem to require the fixing of some criteria by which progress towards the reduction of this problem can be measured.

Taking account of both these aspects of the argument, it is of interest to ascertain the budgetary and trade positions of the Community and its members if exact self-supply were achieved in each product currently in surplus. Under this alternative policy, the Community price levels need to be adjusted so that for each such commodity, the deficits of member-countries whose domestic consumption exceeds production can be exactly met by the combined surpluses of the other members. The elimination of net trade in these agricultural products with the rest of the world (low levels of gross trade with the rest of the world are maintained to reflect current differences between gross and net trade figures) means that export refunds and import levies are considerably reduced, and almost offset each other in the Community budget. However, MCAs and other payments continue, although at different levels, as the pattern of intra-Community trade alters under the different situation.

In columns (1) and (4) of Table 6.2 it is possible to compare the base position of 112 per cent Community self-supply, with the equilibrium position that would result from separate price adjustments in each surplus commodity to achieve exact self-sufficiency. Net trade with the rest of the world is thus reduced, but gross flows still persist (equal in both import and export directions) in the affected products for seasonal, quality and other reasons. The following major points of comparison may be noted:

(i)   Real prices are lowered by an average
        13-14 per cent, although this figure
        hides a wide range of commodity-
        specific changes.

(ii)   Net FEOGA expenditure falls to 2600
        million EUA, mainly as a result of
        falls in export-refund expenditures
        which are otherwise required to re-
        duce commodity surpluses.

(iii)   If the intervention system operates
        as at present, the change in trading
        patterns as members in surplus re-
        orient their supplies away from
        external countries and towards
        deficit-members (such as the United
        Kingdom) results in fairly constant,
        if not increased, storage expendi-
        ture, while a small Community
        surplus is made on MCAs collected as
        levies on trade between the higher-
        priced suppliers to the lower-priced
        consumer countries.

(iv)   The considerable falls in average
        prices necessary to achieve exact
        self-supply in surplus commodities
        results in large changes in both
        producer and consumer welfare. Due
        to the patterns of production and
        consumption in the various commodi-
        ties involved, producer losses
        exceed consumer gains, but the in-
        clusion of taxpayer gains results
        in an overall welfare gain of over
        3000 million EUA to the Community
        as a whole.

The self-sufficiency policy adopted here has some
feature which render the above results less useful
than might at first appear. The commodity-by-
commodity approach requires considerably different
adjustments to be made in price and quantity levels.
A more effective policy achieving the same goal of
a better balance in agricultural trade would permit
surpluses in some products and deficits in others,
though this would not secure the removal of inter-
dependence with world markets which some see as the
main justification of policies aimed at more exact
self-sufficiency. A further aspect, though one
common to all the alternative policies considered
here, is the country-by-country consequences of

self-sufficiency at Community level. Some EC members would no doubt conceive of self-sufficiency as relevant at the national rather than the Community level. Despite these caveats, however, the present simple version of the self-sufficiency policy is of some interest in indicating the direction and magnitude of changes which such an aim would involve.

FREE MARKET

A move to free market conditions for agricultural commodities represents a massive alteration from the current highly interventionist system to a whole; hearted policy of laissez-faire. It does, however, reflect the often-implicit assumption by neo-classical economists that proper (i.e. socially efficient)valuations and balances of production and consumption can only be reached in a 'perfect' competitive market system. The dismantling of all CAP instruments such as MCAs, producer and consumer subsidies, and external-trade refunds and levies would leave production, consumption and trade in the Community exposed to the conditions of the market of which it would be a part. Both farmers and consumers would face competition and opportunities unaffected by the complex set of trading, guarantee and subsidy arrangements at present in force. In a sense, then, the full opportunity costs of CAP will be exhibited by considering a change from the base-position policy to a free market.

One further aspect of importance must be noted. Currently, the CAP is but one of a large number of national and international policies and agreements which affect agriculture throughout most of the sorld. Some countries, such as other West European nations and the United States, maintain strongly protectionist systems for the sake of their domestic farming; others, such as Australia and Canada, are markedly oriented towards international trade. The trade policies of the centrally-planned economies and of the third world also affect the current world market. When considering the abandonment of the CAP, therefore, the position of these parallel policies must be considered. It would possibly be most logical to suppose similar policy changes in most if not all other countries, but these would be often difficult to specify, as well as involving greatly-increased modelling complexity.

Hence the 'free market' policy alternative actually implemented in the present study envisages only the elimination of the CAP itself (strictly, the guarantee section of FEOGA) but the maintenance of

current agricultural policies in non-EC countries,
particularly in the EC's more important trading
partners such as the United States. Although this
alternative is implausible in a real-world policy
sense, it has the merits of conceptual simplicity
and a fundamental economic benchmark, and is therefore included in the present study as a policy
alternative free of the ambiguities which inevitably
surround a more 'realistic' scenario.

The expected financial outcome of such a change
is of course to eliminate budgetary flows altogether.
Production, consumption and trade will react to the
much lower level of commodity prices that would
result, at least for most products, in the event
that the EC aimed for a market with prices set com-
petitively and free of the influences of oligopoly
or trade agreements.

Columns (1) and (5) in Table 6.2 compare the
1980 base position with the free market alternative.
Self-supply falls by 30 percentage points to 82 as a
result of the average 32 per cent fall in product
prices. That this fall is not greater (in view of
the substantial number of products for which 1980
Community prices were at least double the then world
price level) is due to the large price-raising
effect on world markets which would result from the
abandonment of European agricultural protection.
Nevertheless, the net position is of some interest,
despite the necessarily speculative nature of these
results. The welfare effects on producers, consumers and taxpayers also indicates the magnitude of
the discrepancy between the current situation and a
particular theoretical optimum.

DISCUSSION

Table 6.2 as a whole illustrates the enormous range
of choice which faces the analyst (if not the prac-
tising politician) in trying to assess the costs and
benefits of policy changes. In the array of five
policies chosen in this study, the base position
represents a maximum in agricultural protectionism
and public expenditure. This is partly fortuitous,
(since a more protective version of the CAP could
have been easily included), but in time may be seen
to reflect the realities of shifts in Community
agricultural policy fairly well as its development
in the 1970s confronted the realities of budget constraints. Technical progress is outstripping the
capacity of markets to absorb ever-increasing quantities of product, and hard-pressed national exchequers are now looking hard at the extent to which

scarce public funds have been used to insulate the markets from the consequences. Hence the major current concern over the Common Agricultural Policy is the expansion of FEOGA expenditure, and the four alternative policies of Table 6.2 reflect varying degrees of political and theoretical vigour in pursuing this goal.

Naturally many other alternative policies could and should be analysed in the search for acceptable alternatives to the continuance of the present situation. These include: extension of the co-responsibility levy system to both higher rates and over products other than milk; a degree of national financing of some or all expenditure categories; and the imposition of national or other quotas on the production of commodities in surplus[4]. In addition, the impact of various external events on the development of CAP are of interest: the second expansion of the Community to include Greece and other Mediterranean countries; fluctuations in world commodity markets; and possible alterations of historic agricultural trends in such factors as energy usage, farm structure, and genetic improvement. Some of these avenues are being currently followed up within the model framework described above.

NOTES

1. Perhaps the most accessible contemporary descriptions of the 1980 Commission proposals of 31 January 1980 and the package finally adopted by the Council on 28-30 May 1980 are contained in the publications of Agra-Europe (London) Ltd., e.g. '1980/81 Prices', Green Europe, February 1980, pp.15-22, and 'EEC Farm Prices for 1980/81', Green Europe, May 1980, pp.27-30.
2. See, for example, Stocktaking of the Common Agricultural Policy, Directorate-General for Agriculture of the European Communities Commission, Newsletter No. 3, March 1975, para 125. More recently, the Commission's annual proposals for the setting of farm prices have included suggestions for the phasing out of MCAs (see note 1), but these have been regarded as additional negotiating points by most members, and technical problems associated with the administration of the ECU as the central currency of the European Monetary System (EMS) have added to the difficulty of achieving the complete phasing out of MCAs.
3. A good discussion of the arguments for and against self-sufficiency in agriculture is contained in a study by Professor Christopher Ritson,

Self-Sufficiency and Food Security, Centre for Agricultural Strategy Paper 8, University of Reading,
1980. Somewhat more political re-statements of the
self-sufficiency arguments may be found in the two
major policy statements of the United Kingdom government during the 1970s: Food from Our Own Resources,
(Command Paper 6020, 1975) and Farming and the Nation
(Command Paper 7458,1979).
4.   Some of these alternative policy options are
discussed by the authors in 'Some Development
Options for the CAP', in the Journal of Agricultural
Economics, Vol. 32(3), September 1981, and in 'Levy
Policies and EEC Agricultural Surpluses' by Kevin A.
Parton, to appear in Oxford Agrarian Studies 1982,
obtainable from the author at the University of New
England, Armidale, New South Wales, Australia.

Chapter 7

COMMODITY EFFECTS OF POLICY ALTERNATIVES

The previous chapter has described the results of
five agricultural policy simulations at the level of
the Community as a whole. Physical, economic and
financial aspects of these policy alternatives have
all been considered, reflecting the broad concerns
of the Community as a whole about the difficulties
being encountered in pursuing further its Common
Agricultural Policy within tightening budgetary
constraints. However, for a fuller understanding of
the effects of different policies, it is necessary
to analyse each at commodity level. The impact of
the CAP varies significantly from product to product
in the level of protection and subsidy maintained
under current arrangements, with consequences for
the pattern of the income and expenditure flows of
Community agriculture, and there are important interactions between commodities at both the production
and consumption ends of the market. Alternative
policies would have equally striking commodity
effects, which need to be compared with the present
pattern of support. For each of the major commodity
groups, this chapter outlines their importance within EC agriculture as a whole and describes the major
market and budget features under the selected types
of policy.

CEREALS

Cereals occupy a central position in nearly all
farming systems, including those which operate within a rich, highly developed economy such as the EC.
Direct human consumption of cereals may tend to fall
as incomes rise, and consumers switch to higher-
value livestock products, but this in itself tends to
increase demand for cereals (of different types) for
use in animal feeding. Being easy to store and
transport, cereals also play an important role in
agricultural trade, and the size and reliability of

101

the North American sources of cereals have encouraged the development in Europe of large-scale farming enterprises dependent on these imported feedgrains.

The total area of cereals in the European Community in 1979 was 26.7 million ha. or 28.7 per cent of the utilized agricultural area, being of greatest significance in France, Germany and Denmark, in contrast to Ireland and the Netherlands where grass and fodder crops are more prevalent. Barley area slightly exceeds that of common wheat at nearly 10 million ha. each, with maize about 3 million ha.. Durum wheat, rye and meslin, oats and other cereals comprise the remainder of the total area. The Community now appears to be moving into a structural surplus in total cereals at production levels around 115 million tonnes.

The basis of the current CAP cereals market organisation was developed in the 1960s as the original six member states harmonised their separate systems towards the (high) German price levels. Under the present system, as laid down in EC Regulation 2729/75, and later additions, the target price, representing the desired market price at the point of greatest deficit (Duisburg in West Germany), is supported by a slightly lower threshold price for imports (maintained by variable import levies), and an intervention price for Community-produced grain which, unless removed from the market, would lower cereal prices to unacceptable levels. For breadmaking wheat there is a corresponding reference price. All these prices are increased in monthly steps throughout most of the cereal marketing year (1 August to 31 July). Recently, the Community has attempted to alter the relationship between the level of price support for cereals of different types, so as to avoid the accumulation of wheat surpluses, while imports of feedgrains and cereal substitutes such as manioc, oilcakes and food industry byproducts have been growing.

In 1980, total Community expenditure on cereals under the CAP was about 1600 million EUA (or 16 per cent of FEOGA Guarantee expenditure), of which 1100 million EUA went as export refunds, and 500 million EUA on intervention payments such as production subsidies (e.g. aid for durum wheat in Italy) and storage payments. Considerable growth has occurred under some of these headings, however, and a combination of good Community harvest and low world prices could increase the total still further.

Table 7.1 shows the major results for the cereals concerned in the present study - common wheat,

Table 7.1 : Cereals[a] : Community-Level Policy Comparisons.

Item	1980 Base Position	1980 Price Package	Price Harmonisation	Community Self-Sufficiency	Free Market[b]
Self-supply (index):	112	110	111	100	118
Real price change (%):	0.0	-4.4	-2.5	-20.7	-26.8
FEOGA Budgetary Flows (mEUA):					
- export refunds	1008	723	977	277	0
- intervention	261	257	260	245	0
- MCAs	40	30	0	-47	0
- gross expenditure	1309	1011	1237	475	0
- income	-745	-642	-665	-291	0
- net expenditure	564	368	571	184	0
Balance of Trade (mEUA)	1626	276	1527	0	2091
Welfare Effects of Policy Changes (mEUA):					
- producers	0	-826	-494	-3730	-5251
- consumers	0	245	228	-386	1382

a. Common wheat, durum, barley, oats, rye and meslin, and maize.

b. 'Community Self-Sufficiency' means that, for each surplus product separately, production equals utilization. However, minimum gross trade flows are maintained, so that export refunds and import levies still appear in this table.

durum wheat, barley, rye and meslin, and maize.
Ceteris paribus, the 1980 price package avoided[*] an
average real cereal price decline of four to five
per cent which would have resulted in a substantial
reduction in net expenditure on exports of cereals
under the CAP. On the other hand, harmonisation to
common prices has a very limited effect on the
Community's budget despite the slightly lower average price level which such a move would entail.
Attainment of self-sufficiency in surplus products
greatly reduces net expenditure on cereals, although
the pattern of intra- and extra-Community trade
(maintaining minimal trade levels) is considerably
different. The first and third of these alternative
policies have a marked effect on the Community's
balance of trade with third countries, as of course
does a free market in agricultural products, through
larger quantities of imports being available at
lower prices. Except for harmonisation, the alternative policies severely penalise producers in comparison with the base position (the 1980 price
package seems to have been heavily weighted against
cereal producers), and the gains to (non-farm) consumers after adjustment to all price changes are not
sufficient to offset these losses.

MILK PRODUCTS

Despite the stability of dairy cow numbers in the
Community at around 25 million, dairy farming has
presented one of the most difficult areas of the CAP.
Remorseless changes in farm structure and technical
improvements have raised total milk production to
nearly 100 million tonnes. Overall Community self-
sufficiency in milk is now permanently over-achieved,
which means that milk products such as butter and
skimmed milk powder have been in embarrassing surplus.
Some of this can be absorbed as animal feed, but the
rest has either been stored or exported, often at
considerable cost. Attempts to improve the situation through economic instruments, such as lower
real prices, have been hampered by the large number
of small milk producers whose incomes would be severely affected by such measures. There have, therefore, been strenuous efforts to ameliorate the situation in the longer term by financing schemes to encourage producers to leave dairy farming, and strong
pressure to limit competition with competitive products such as margarine.

[*] See Chapter 6 (p.89); the figures for this policy
estimate the 'no-agreement' outcome in 1980.

The common organisation of the market in dairy products is operated mainly at the ports and at the level of first-time buyers (usually co-operatives or, in the United Kingdom, the milk marketing boards). Variable levies, export refunds and intervention buying of butter and skimmed milk powder are supplemented by a wide variety of storage aids, subsidies to industrial users and special consumer groups, and food aid programmes. Since 1977, co-responsibility levies, as a percentage of the target price, have been payable on most milk produced within the Community, and there have been attempts to reduce the import quotas on butter guaranteed to New Zealand.

FEOGA guarantee expenditure on milk products in 1980 was just under 5000 million EUA (42 per cent of the total), of which export refunds required about 2600 million EUA and intervention (mainly aids for skimmed milk powder) the rest. Milk producers, through the levy scheme, contributed about 200 million EUA towards this cost. Public stocks of skimmed milk powder have been considerably reduced, but butter is again accumulating in store.

The changes brought about by a switch of policy towards alternative goals are illustrated in Table 7.2. The overall effect of the 1980 price package (which awarded relatively lower rates of nominal price increases to milk products but accompanied this with a decreased co-responsibility levy on milk) brings some reduction in the self-supply ratio, but is more effective in its budgetary impact, reducing net expenditure by twenty per cent. Price harmonisation has a similar effect on the levels of self-supply and net budget expenditure. Both alternatives involve almost offsetting gains and losses to producers and consumers of about 600 million EUA.

The massive policy changes involved in achieving exact Community self-sufficiency in each milk product, or free-market conditions in these products, have much greater impacts. Self-sufficiency drives net expenditure down to a fifth of its base level conditions, and involves massive loss (3000 million EUA) to producers (despite the lower cost of cereal feed), only partly offset by a 2000 million EUA gain to non-farm consumers. The even more drastic shift, to free-market conditions, results in nearly halved average price levels, a trade deficit of over 5000 million EUA, and producer losses and consumer gains of 7000-8000 million EUA. Naturally there is much uncertainty over these magnitudes, since the conditions of trade and storage policies can only be

Table 7.2 : Milk Products[a] : Community Level Policy Comparisons.

Item	1980 Base Position	1980 Price Package	Price Harmonisation	Community Self-Sufficiency[b]	Free Market
Self-supply (index):	151	145	144	100	72
Real price change (%):	0.0	-3.3	-3.0	-22.3	-43.3
FEOGA Budgetary Flows (mEUA):					
- export refunds	4147	3699	3847	277	0
- intervention	648	648	637	554	0
- MCAs	153	145	0	-32	0
- gross expenditure	4947	4492	4484	1404	0
- income	-511	-822	-778	-575	0
- net expenditure	4435	3670	3706	828	0
Balance of Trade (mEUA)	1372	1252	1217	0	-4902
Welfare Effects of Policy Changes (mEUA):					
- producers	0	-615	-641	-3079	-6919
- consumers	0	518	612	2160	8089

a. Butter, cheese, skimmed milk powder (SMP), cream, and condensed milk.

b. See Note b to Table 7.1.

roughly estimated for policies so radically different from the present ones. On the other hand, the
figures indicate the size of the financial and economic welfare gains that are potentially available in
attempts to reformulate policy for these products.

LIVESTOCK PRODUCTS OTHER THAN MILK

Livestock production takes place on the majority of
Community farms, but the methods employed vary
greatly between regions and between the farms themselves. At one end of the spectrum, producers of
intensive livestock such as pigs and poultry are engaged in a capital-intensive high-throughput enter-
prise heavily dependent on cereals for feedingstuffs,
whether grown on the same farm or purchased from
elsewhere. At the other extreme, farmers on marginal
land (less-favoured areas in the jargon of the
Community[1]) often run extensive and flexible systems
of animal grazing, although their output pattern may
be heavily affected by adverse weather conditions
and unexpected winter feeding problems.
        Corresponding to these variations, the common
market organisation in livestock products varies considerably from commodity to commodity, and has developed in different ways as new pressures - political, technical and financial - have come to bear on
the system. The livestock products covered
in this study are beef and veal, and pigmeat,
poultrymeat and eggs. Sheepmeat has recently been
brought into the ambit of the CAP[2] but is not included here, although with the accession of Greece,
this group of products will no doubt become more important, especially in a regional context.
        Table 7.3 shows the results for all livestock
products other than milk. The results will be discussed in more detail in the sub-sections below on
beef and veal, and on pig and poultry products, but
Table 7.3 should be compared with Tables 7.1 and 7.2
to realise the much lower expenditures which are en-
tailed by the Community's market organisation in
these products. Nevertheless, policy moves in this
area are as significant as those elsewhere, particularly when the important cereal/livestock links
(reflected in the calculations - see p.83) are combined.

Beef and Veal

Community markets in beef and veal are protected by
a series of measures ranging from intervention buying, private storage aid, third-country trading

Table 7.3 : Non-Milk Livestock Products[a] : Community Level Policy Comparisons.

Item	1980 Base Position	1980 Price Package	Price Harmonisation	Community Self-Sufficiency[b]	Free Market
Self-supply (index) :	102	99	100	100	72
Real price change (%):	0.0	-4.7	-3.0	-13.6	-38.6
FEOGA Budgetary Flows (mEUA):					
- export refunds	598	471	550	670	0
- intervention	308	295	292	288	0
- MCAs	-94	-97	0	-75	0
- gross expenditure	812	669	843	884	0
- income	-677	-978	-839	-264	0
- net expenditure	134	-309	4	620	0
Balance of Trade (mEUA)	542	53	171	0	-6625
Welfare Effects of Policy Changes (mEUA):					
- producers	0	-1173	-815	-1943	-8839
- consumers	0	1596	1284	4594	14477

a.   Beef and veal, pigmeat, poultrymeat and eggs.

b.   See Note b to Table 7.1.

agreements and variable production premia resembling
deficiency payments. The complexity of the measures
is due to the wide fluctuations experienced on the
markets for these products, and the heterogeneity of
production and marketing systems for cattle. The
Community is almost self-sufficient in beef and veal
overall but this disguises substantial trade flows in
the various processed meat products.

     Table 7.4 compares the calculated outcomes of
the five policies for beef and veal. Comparing the
1980 base position to that without the 1980 price
package, the alternative depresses real prices by
five per cent, reduces self-sufficiency from 97 to
93, and halves net budgetary expenditure on these
products. A move to price harmonisation slightly
decreases average real prices in the Community, but
reduces expenditure on these products by a similar
amount. Community self-sufficiency in surplus products requires no change in the average real price
of beef and veal but permits small reductions in the
financial magnitudes involved. Free market conditions cut self-sufficiency to less than 50 per cent,
with price declines of over 30 per cent. In terms
of the net effects on producers and consumers, after
allowance for cheaper feed cereals, the 1980 price
package and harmonisation show net gains of 100-150
million EUA, helps producers considerably, and free
market conditions show large net gains, albeit at
large and probably unsupportable cost to livestock
producers. However, this last result does illustrate how the lower real cereal prices which follow
from moves towards freer-market conditions help to
soften somewhat the direct effects of lower livestock
product prices.

Pigs and Poultry

The production of pigmeat, poultrymeat and eggs in
the Community is mainly protected by a system of
levies on third-country imports of these products in
which the EC is not in serious surplus. Actual
intervention on EC markets takes place only for pigmeat, and is much more indirect than for cereals and
milk. The market regime attempts to stabilise production without leading to excessive storage stocks,
and support prices are related to those for cereals
as the major input cost.

     The base position for pig and poultry products
shows a negative level of net FEOGA guarantee expenditure, since import levies and MCA income offset
the export refunds necessary to dispose of the
slight surplus which the Community enjoys. Without

Table 7.4 : Beef and Veal : Community Level Policy Comparisons.

Item	1980 Base Position	1980 Price Package	Price Harmonisation	Community Self-Sufficiency[a]	Free Market
Production (m tonnes):	6.1	5.8	5.8	5.6	3.1
Utilisation (m tonnes):	6.2	6.3	6.3	5.9	6.6
Self-supply (index):	97	93	93	95	47
Real price change (%):	0.0	-4.0	-2.7	0.0	-34.0
FEOGA Budgetary Flows (mEUA):					
- export refunds	105	60	66	67	0
- intervention	300	287	284	277	0
- MCAs	15	4	0	9	0
- gross expenditure	419	351	350	354	0
- income	-132	-245	-239	-175	0
- net expenditure	287	106	112	179	0
Balance of Trade (mEUA)	-136	-384	-362	-247	-3437
Welfare Effects of Policy Changes (mEUA):					
- producers	0	-234	-193	833	-1588
- consumers	0	373	288	0	3286

a. In all surplus products separately, maintaining minimum trade levels with third countries.

Table 7.5 : Pigs and Poultry[a] : Community Level Policy Comparisons.

Item	1980 Base Price	1980 Price Package	Price Harmonisation	Community Self-Sufficiency[b]	Free Market[b]
Self-supply (index) :	107	105	107	100	85
Real price change (%) :	0.0	-5.0	-3.0	-20.0	-30.0
FEOGA Budgetary Flows (mEUA):					
- export refunds	493	411	484	604	0
- intervention	8	8	8	10	0
- MCAs	-108	-109	0	-84	0
- gross expenditure	393	317	492	530	0
- income	-545	-732	-600	-177	0
- net expenditure	-153	-415	-108	442	0
Balance of Trade (mEUA)	678	437	533	0	-3188
Welfare Effects of Policy Changes (mEUA):					
- producers	0	-938	-622	-2776	-7251
- consumers	0	1222	997	4594	11192

a. Pigmeat, poultrymeat and eggs.

b. See Note b to Table 7.1.

the 1980 price package, there would have been lower
real prices and, ceteris paribus, further Community
income, although at considerable cost to producers.
Harmonisation to slightly lower average common
prices has the reverse effect but, due to the
pattern of production, consumption and MCAs, still
manages to benefit consumers more than producers.
Community self-sufficiency in each surplus product
involves substantial net expenditure and large
opposite effects on producers and consumers. A free
market also offers net welfare gains but at much
lower prices and with negative balance of trade
effects.

SUGAR

The production of sugar in the European Community is
a striking example of how agricultural protectionism
can, over a number of years, substantially alter the
pattern of production and trade. Domestic beet
sugar from Community farms has been steadily dis-
placing imported cane sugar and, indeed, competing
with such sugar on world markets. Some of the best
farm land in the Community is devoted to the beet
crop, and a considerable processing industry has
grown up in these areas. The Community has undertaken to guarantee access to a certain quantity of
cane sugar from the ACP countries each year under
the Lomé agreement but this has not allayed the
fears of these nations that they will be slowly
forced out of the market (mainly the United Kingdom).
In addition, consumption levels in the Community
have been falling since the shortages of the mid-
1970s, and there are threats of competition from
iso-glucose and other manufactured sweeteners.
     The CAP support system for sugar differs some-
what from that used to date for other commodities.
Although target, intervention and threshold prices
are fixed in the usual way, the derived guarantee
prices are payable only for basic 'A' quota tonnages
of processed sugar allocated to each beet refinery
from a fixed Community total. Above this level, up
to a maximum 'B' quota which is determined annually,
sugar supplies are subject to a production levy of
up to 30 per cent of the relevant intervention price.
Sugar produced in excess of the maximum 'B' quota is
not price supported. With increasing yields, the
Community in the 1970s has usually been in surplus
with prices well above world levels. However, the
volatile world sugar market has occasionally resulted
in the protection of the Community's domestic consumers against unusually high world prices by the

Table 7.6 : Sugar : Community Level Policy Comparisons.

Item	1980 Base Position	1980 Price Package	Price Harmonisation	Community Self-Sufficiency[b]	Free Market
Production (m tonnes):	11.4	11.1	11.2	10.0	11.1
Utilisation (m tonnes):	8.9	9.1	9.0	10.0	10.0
Self-supply (index):	128	121	124	100	111
Real price change (%):	0.0	-5.5	-2.8	-20.4	-20.4
FEOGA Budgetary Flows (mEUA):					
- export refunds	408	250	374	-33	0
- intervention	185	180	183	162	0
- MCAs	41	32	0	-8	0
- gross expenditure	635	463	557	121	0
- incomea	-278	-196	-237	30	0
- net expenditure	356	266	320	151	0
Balance of Trade (mEUA)	846	665	754	0	395
Welfare Effects of Policy Changes (mEUA):					
- producers	0	-265	-152	-973	-1030
- consumers	0	214	142	863	888

a. There is little levy income from sugar imports under the Lomé agreement, and the bulk of this income is producer levy.

b. See Note b to Table 7.1.

use of export levies. In 1980,FEOGA guarantee expenditure on sugar totalled about 700 million EUA,
of which 400 million EUA went on export refunds, and
most of the rest on storage subsidies. Sugar levies,
accruing to the Community budget, amounted to about
500 million EUA.
      Table 7.6 illustrates the effects of the various
modelled policy alternatives on the base 1980 position which reflects a Community surplus of about 30
per cent. The 1980 price package avoided an average
real price decline for sugar and a lowering of the
self-supply index to 121. Net budgetary costs are
little affected, since gains on reduced export refunds are almost offset by decreased levies from
producers, who are quite severely penalised in comparison with consumer gains. Price harmonisation
involves a slight fall in average real prices but
the different production and consumption patterns
result in some lowering of the overall level of
self-supply. However net Community expenditure on
sugar remains almost unaltered, and such a policy
change has little net effect on the economic position of sugar producers or consumers.
      Exact Community self-sufficiency in sugar can
only be achieved with a 20 per cent drop in real
prices. The effect on the world market (under the
conditions explained in Chapter 6) is also dramatic,
with world prices rising above Community levels,
reversing the budgetary flows on third-country imports and exports (as occurred in 1974). The
budgetary burden thus shifts from export refund subsidies to import subsidies, and if storage aid continues on a similar basis as at present there is
still a net cost. The massive, but opposite, changes
in the economic surplus position of producers and
consumers almost exactly cancel each other out.
Under free trade, Community sugar prices drop by
the same percentage, but the absence of the producer
levy limits the fall of the self-supply inded to 111.
Although budgetary costs are eliminated, the economic
balance between producers and consumers is altered
by about 1000 million EUA in either direction.

CONCLUSIONS

The above, commodity by commodity, analysis of the
effects of implementing various alternative policies
for EC agriculture has attempted to quantify some of
the problems and opportunities facing politicians
and administrators who are trying to reform the CAP.
None of the alternatives included in the present
analysis emerges as a definite improvement for all

114

groups over the existing situation, but this is not surprising since the search for such a policy has gone on fruitlessly for several years. A final judgement on the overall ranking of each option has to involve a weighted assessment of the benefits and costs imposed on the various interest groups involved, and can only be arrived at in a framework of politics and negotiation.

Table 7.7 brings together the welfare effects of moving from the base policy situation to each of the four specified alternatives, disaggregated by the commodity groups discussed above for producers, consumers (outside agriculture) and taxpayers (as represented by changes in net FEOGA expenditure on each commodity group from the base position. It will be noted that the effect of the 1980 price package involves roughly equivalent producer losses and consumer gains in livestock products and sugar, but penalised cereal producers with much less gain to the non-farming community. Without the package taxpayers gain, as they are required to contribute less to the financing of the policy with respect to these products, particularly in milk. Elimination of MCAs through harmonisation to common EUA prices has a somewhat smaller overall effect, and mainly benefits the consumption of milk products and pig and poultry products (through lower prices in countries whose positive MCAs lead to higher prices in the base situation). Community self-sufficiency in products in surplus in 1980 has major negative implications for most producers, although beef production is actually aided by the cheaper cereals that would result from such a policy. Consumers would correspondingly benefit, except in cereals, where alternative farm uses of these products are available and taxpayers actually lose out as far as pig and poultry products are concerned. Milk is the major commodity for which self-sufficiency holds out large taxpayer savings. A free market re-emphasises the pre-eminence of milk as the potential source of net benefits, although the situation in other livestock products should not be ignored even if taxpayer involvement is lower. The availability of cheaper cereals and the release of resources from milk production would, on this analysis, greatly benefit consumption, at a cost to producers which is some 2800 million EUA lower. This should give some scope for negotiated policy movement in order to capture at least some of these potential net gains.

Perhaps the major feature of the tables presented in this chapter is that, although many policy changes involve large or very large changes in the

Table 7.7 : Commodity Groups : Community Level Policy Comparisons of Welfare Effects.

Item	1980 Price Package	Price Harmonisation	Community Self-Sufficiency[a]	Free Market
Welfare Effects (mEUA) on:				
Producers:				
Cereals	-826	-494	-3730	-5251
Milk Products	-615	-641	-3079	-6919
Beef and Veal	-234	-193	833	-1588
Pigs and Poultry	-938	-622	-2776	-7251
Sugar	-265	-152	-973	-1030
Total:	-2879	-2102	-9725	-22039
Consumers:				
Cereals	245	228	-386	1382
Milk Products	518	612	2160	8089
Beef and Veal	373	288	0	3286
Pigs and Poultry	1222	997	4594	11192
Sugar	214	142	863	888
Total:	2573	2267	7231	24836
Taxpayers:				
Cereals	196	-7	380	564
Milk Products	765	729	3607	4435
Beef and Veal	181	175	108	287
Pigs and Poultry	262	-45	-595	-153
Sugar	90	36	205	356
Total:	1494	888	3705	5489

a. See Note b to Table 7.1.

economic situation of producers and consumers, the
net changes are small or trivial by comparison.
Policies which result in large net losses to producer and consumer groups as a whole are likely to
be accompanied by decreased taxpayer burdens which
in magnitude completely or partially offset these
losses. More generally net overall gains to society
from a policy move are nearly always less than
losses to at least one party. This awkward feature
of the economic system to which the CAP is applied
explains much of the difficulty of finding politically acceptable directions of reform.

NOTES

1.   Directive 75/268 of the Community permits additional aid to farmers in certain regions of member
states, known generally as less favoured areas. The
aim is to maintain the economy and population of
regions which suffer particular handicaps of
climate, terrain or distance from markets. About
twenty per cent of the total agricultural area of
the Community, and about thirteen per cent of all
farmers, are affected.
2.   Regulation 1837/80 of June 20, 1980, defines
the Common Organisation of the Market in Sheepmeat
and Goatmeat, and has been in effect since the
autumn of that year.

Chapter 8

COUNTRY EFFECTS OF POLICY ALTERNATIVES

This chapter analyses the results reported in Chapter 6, disaggregated to the level of the member states of the Community. In doing so, it will become apparent why certain countries take up the attitudes they do in respect of moves in the direction of the policy alternatives considered. For those who support the Community idea, these cross-currents will be seen as problems which the CAP should be designed to help resolve against a background of mutual economic co-operation between members. Their opponents will interpret the figures as illustrations of the fundamental flaws in the concept of the Community, and may expect the strains set up eventually to cause the break-up of the CAP, if not the Community as a whole. Whatever view is taken, country-specific effects seem of vital importance in understanding past and present developments in policy.

GERMANY

A mixture of motives has ensured the active involvement of Germany in the European Community ever since its inception in 1958. The desire to re-establish its industrial and political position within Europe was one of the strongest of these motives. The unquestionable achievement of this aim owes a great deal to the economic framework provided by the European Communities. In addition, Germany's overall deficit in agricultural products made attractive the idea of a close relationship with its major producer neighbours of France, the Netherlands, and Denmark, and has enabled German farmers to enjoy high levels of protection, enhanced since 1971 by an undervalued green mark. The combination of high farm prices and widespread industrial development has transformed German agriculture into a highly productive industry with plentiful capital supplies and a large amount of part-time farming by wage- and salary-earners. Supported by a favourable political configuration, the country's agriculture has steadily increased output, driving up the self-supply index in most products. The success of the rest of the economy has so far been able to bear the financial consequences both for taxpayers and consumers, with spare capacity for shouldering a good deal of the Community budget for expenditure on common policies in other member states.

Table 8.1 shows the effects of alternative policies on the equilibrium 1980 agricultural position of West Germany. In the base situation, the country has almost achieved self-sufficiency in the farm products included in this study. Gross FEOGA expenditure within its borders is about 2400 million EUA (about a fifth of the total Community expenditure), mainly on surplus disposal, while budgetary income from agricultural sources is only 500 million EUA (19 per cent of total Community FEOGA income), leaving a net expenditure figure of 1800 million EUA. If member states were to finance this expenditure on the same percentage basis as they contributed custom duties and VAT receipts in 1980, then West Germany's contribution towards the agricultural budget is 2700 million EUA leaving a balance of FEOGA payments of 900 million EUA. It should be remembered that this latter figure cannot be directly compared with published data from the Commission since we are here only concerned with the FEOGA sector of the budget and its separate financing. Together with its 'private' trade deficit of 1500 million EUA, Germany's overall agricultural payments balance is thus just over 2400 million EUA (a figure which would no doubt increase if non-CAP products imported from third countries were included). Compared to the situation where the country 'nationalises' its agricultural policy, maintaining domestic prices through retained import levies and self-financed export subsidies, there is an estimated trade loss of over 800 million EUA (on high-priced imports) and an overall loss of 1700 million EUA after inclusion of FEOGA contributions less expenditure. These figures are large, but as potential gains are presumably seen as unobtainable without even greater costs in terms of European economic disintegration were such a policy adopted. Overall, these results confirm Germany's position as a major contributor to Community funds, as well as a large recipient of expenditure incurred on account of commodities in overall surplus.

Table 8.1 : Germany : Policy Comparisons

Item	1980 Base Position	1980 Price Package	Price Harmonisation	Community Self-Sufficiency	Free Market
Self-supply (index):	96	93	89	86	63
Real price change (%):	0.0	-4.3	-9.8	-13.5	-38.3
FEOGA Budgetary Flows (mEUA):					
- gross expenditure	12437	2144	2044	475	0
- income	-617	-810	-739	-260	0
- net expenditure	1820	1334	1305	215	0
- VAT contribution	2707	1986	2300	854	0
Balances and Effects (mEUA):					
- of FEOGA payments	-887	-652	-995	-638	0
- of trade	-1513	-1692	-2449	-2289	-5345
- of agric. payments	-2400	-2344	-3444	-2927	-5345
- pref. trade effect	-853	-729	-1113	-519	0
- budget and trade effect	-1740	-1381	-2108	-1157	0
Welfare Effects of Policy Changes (mEUA):					
- producers	0	-750	-1690	-2546	-6496
- consumers	0	817	1857	2450	9017
- taxpayers	0	721	407	1854	2707
- overall	0	789	575	1757	5228

Alternative policies have a varied effect on the patterns described above. A with/without simulation of the 1980 price package leads, after equilibrium, to a small drop in FEOGA expenditure (following a 4 per cent fall in Germany's farm prices), but a rise in Community income from agricultural levies reduces net expenditure in Germany by about a quarter. Moreover, the effects in other member states of decreased farm prices leads to a market fall in the financial contribution required, and the overall FEOGA deficit falls from nearly 900 million EUA to 650 million EUA. Other effects on payments balances and on economic welfare reflect the essentially financial impact of the 1980 agreement on Germany's situation within the CAP. Harmonisation to common prices involves a 10 per cent drop in German farm prices as positive MCAs are removed, and reduces self-supply index to 89. The overall budgetary impact on the country of such a Community policy is adverse since expenditure within Germany falls by a sixth, with a consequent decrease in net agricultural expenditure, although the national financial contribution to the Community budget deficit also falls somewhat. Hence the overall (negative) balance on agriculture rises to 1000 million EUA, though consumers gain marginally over producers. A policy of Community self-sufficiency in each commodity in surplus in 1980 has similar but larger physical and price effects to that of price harmonisation. The elimination of export refunds (except on residual trade commitments) and a fall in import levies, reduces net agricultural expenditure by the Community inside Germany to 200 million EUA, only a ninth of the base figure. However, contributions to finance expenditure elsewhere keep the overall balance to over 600 million EUA. Removal of the CAP as a whole has of course a drastic effect on German agriculture, with an average real price fall of 38 per cent and self-supply down to 63 index points. The elimination of Community budgetary flows would hardly compensate for such a traumatic experience, but the figures are still of interest as an indication of the level of protection enjoyed by the Community's highest-priced agricultural producers.

FRANCE

As the Community's largest agricultural producer, responsible for about 30 per cent of total production, France has always enjoyed a special position within the development of the CAP. In addition to

her importance in terms of size, France also encompasses a wide variety of farming, from 'northern'
cereal and livestock enterprises to 'southern' products such as wine, olive oil, fruit and vegetables.
Although a staunch supporter of the CAP system
(which was largely designed under French influence),
France has never fought shy of acting with determination in defence of national interests, even to the
point of withdrawing from the administrative machinery of the Community.

Table 8.2 shows that in the base policy simulation, France enjoys a self-supply index of 126 and
gross FEOGA expenditure within her borders of 2600
million EUA. Her financial contribution largely
offsets this sum, but the healthy balance of trade
surplus in agricultural products leaves the country
enjoying an overall balance of agricultural payments
of 3000 million EUA.

Under alternative policies, France experiences
a variety of effects. The 1980 price package
avoided a four per cent real average price fall,
left the overall FEOGA balance undisturbed, but reduced the balance of trade surplus. Elimination of
France's negative MCAs raises prices by four per
cent and again leads to offsetting financial effects,
but this time the balance of trade improves still
further. Minimisation of surplus products for the
Community would, in the conditions of 1980, be
deleterious for France's agricultural producers, but
benefit her consumers and taxpayers through lower
prices and much lower financial contributions. Free
market conditions for the EC drive the French self-
supply index just below 100.

ITALY

Until the accession of Greece, Italy undoubtedly
felt somewhat isolated as the only fully Mediterranean member of the European Communities. Protection
for her specialist products has tended to lag behind
that of milk, beef and cereals, and although special
arrangements such as producer subsidies for durum
wheat and olive oil have been made to safeguard the
incomes of the small and poor Italian farmers, this
has not prevented a sense of partial neglect of
Italian interests within the CAP, nor prevented undesirable situations such as the border 'war' over
wine between France and Italy in 1976. However, it
already seems likely that Italy's attitude is hard-
ening with Greece inside the Community, and Spain
and Portugal awaiting entry, and future developments
of the CAP will have to reflect the new political

Table 8.2 : France : Policy Comparisons

Item	1980 Base Position	1980 Price Package	Price Harmonisation	Community Self-Sufficiency	Free Market
Self-supply (index):	126	122	126	113	100
Real price change (%):	0.0	-4.3	0.0	-12.8	-28.3
FEOGA Budgetary Flows (mEUA):					
- gross expenditure	2614	2137	2537	800	0
- income	-312	-377	-353	-69	0
- net expenditure	2301	1759	2184	732	0
- VAT contribution	2037	1494	1730	-642	0
Balances and Effects (mEUA):					
- of FEOGA payments	265	265	453	89	0
- of trade	2765	2412	2866	1623	17
- of agric. payments	3030	2677	3320	1713	17
- pref. trade effects	-301	-374	-234	-440	0
- budget and trade effect	-36	-109	219	-351	0
Welfare Effects of Policy Changes (mEUA):					
- producers	0	-748	0	-2392	-5198
- consumers	0	573	0	1488	5374
- taxpayers	0	543	307	1394	2037
- overall	0	367	307	491	2213

Table 8.3 : Italy : Policy Comparisons

Item	1980 Base Position	1980 Price Package	Price Harmonisation	Community Self-Sufficiency	Free Market
Self-sufficiency (index):	83	80	83	81	66
Real price change (%):	0.0	-4.3	0.0	-9.4	-27.7
FEOGA Budgetary Flows (mEUA):					
- gross expenditure	1636	1365	1602	1034	0
- income	-708	-1011	-944	-298	0
- net expenditure	927	354	659	735	0
- VAT contribution	900	660	764	284	0
Balance and Effects (mEUA):					
- of FEOGA payments	28	-306	-105	452	0
- of trade	-1943	-1951	-1781	-2111	-3210
- of agric. payments	-1920	-2257	-1886	-1660	-3210
- pref. trade effect	-961	-764	-795	-698	0
- budget and trade effect	-933	-1070	-900	-246	0
Welfare Effects of Policy Changes (mEUA):					
- producers	0	-370	0	-768	-2542
- consumers	0	461	0	879	3863
- taxpayers	0	240	135	616	900
- overall	0	331	135	727	2220

Table 8.4 : Netherlands : Policy Comparisons

Item	1980 Base Position	1980 Price Package	Price Harmonisation	Community Self-Sufficiency	Free Market
Self-supply (index):	216	209	213	189	135
Real price change (%):	0.0	-1.4	-1.8	-14.7	-36.2
FEOGA Budgetary Flows (mEUA):					
- gross expenditure	1672	1508	1510	638	0
- income	-372	-323	-354	-226	0
- net expenditure	1300	1185	1156	411	0
- VAT contribution	500	367	425	158	0
Balance and Effects (mEUA):					
- of FEOGA payments	800	819	732	253	0
- of trade	2481	2299	2470	2208	809
- of agric. payments	3281	3118	3202	2462	809
- pref. trade effect	1146	1001	1132	862	0
- budget and trade effect	1946	1820	1864	1115	0
Welfare Effects of Policy Changes (mEUA):					
- producers	0	-265	-116	-1127	-2213
- consumers	0	125	51	324	1147
- taxpayers	0	133	75	342	500
- overall	0	-7	11	-460	-566

groupings that will become possible.[1]

Table 8.3 shows Italy in almost exact balance over FEOGA-related payments, but suffering a 1900 million EUA balance of trade deficit on the agricultural products included in the present study. Without the 1980 price package, there would have been a decline in real average farm prices in Italy. The corresponding simulation reduces net FEOGA expenditure by two-thirds as production contracts and imports rise accordingly, more than offsetting a lower financial contribution. An unchanged trade balance results in a worsening of the overall payments deficit on the agricultural account. Removal of MCAs, however, would slightly improve the financial position as would Community self-sufficiency in surplus products, which involves a price fall for Italian farmers but quite large gains to consumers and taxpayers. Even free market conditions for the EC do not lead to such a large price decline in Italy as elsewhere, although the trade balance naturally deteriorates.

NETHERLANDS

The Netherlands, like France, has a high degree of dependence on agriculture compared to other West European countries. Its high-value output of vegetables, meat and milk products on a small land area makes it a powerful advocate of developments within the CAP which encourage intensive agricultural production with high input requirements. The country also occupies a special position as the location of major ports for trade both between members of the Community and with much of the rest of the world.

Table 8.4 shows the Netherlands' highly favourable position vis-a-vis the CAP, enjoying high levels of FEOGA expenditure, relatively low financial contributions and a 2500 million EUA surplus on agricultural trade. Its situation under alternative policies reflects this basis. The 'alternative' 1980 price package means only a small real price decline with little change in most financial indicators. Taxpayers benefit from reduced FEOGA expenditures elsewhere, but the impact on producers is enough to offset the other welfare effects. MCA elimination has a similar effect. However, a policy of Community self-sufficiency in surplus products would disadvantage the Netherlands, mainly through the effect on the milk market, and free market conditions would result in an even more serious situation.

BELGIUM/LUXEMBOURG

As small countries, Belgium and Luxembourg have not
played an important part in the formulation of the
CAP, being no doubt content to enjoy the political
and commercial benefits of containing the power
centres of a stable Community of their larger neighbours. Table 8.5 shows that Belgium and Luxembourg
pay an agricultural price for this position, through
a 200 million EUA deficit on the overall FEOGA
account, but this is offset by a positive balance of
agricultural trade. The small price changes involved in the 1980 price package or in the elimination of MCAs would not much affect this basic position. Community self-sufficiency in surplus products
leads to a deterioration in the balance of trade but
a positive FEOGA payments balance. Free trade,
though hitting producers hard, would more than compensate consumers and taxpayers, with an overall
welfare gain of 260 million EUA.

UNITED KINGDOM

Since its accession to the Community in 1973, the
United Kingdom (UK) has always presented special
problems for the operation of the CAP. Although
representing a large consumer market for surplus con-
tinental production, the UK possesses a politically
powerful and unusually-structured agriculture, and
strong external trading links, which have required
special consideration in the design of Community
market organisations and intervention mechanisms.
At a more general level, the 1975 re-negotiations,
after a change of UK government, the unforeseen and
large variations in the value of sterling since 1973,
and the 1979 Conservative government's insistence on
a revised financial mechanism, have all placed un-
usual strains on the Community. It can certainly
not be taken for granted even that UK membership of a
reformed CAP will continue under changing domestic
political alignments.
        Table 8.6 shows part of the source of the prob-
lem. In the base position, FEOGA expenditure in the
UK is completely offset by import and other levies
on agricultural products, even before the VAT contribution of 1400 million EUA is taken into account.[2]
Together with an equal trade deficit, the UK is
clearly paying a high price for Community membership.
This is reinforced by the calculation that an extra
460 million EUA is being paid for high-priced Community imports over and above world price levels.

128

Table 8.5 : Belgium/Luxembourg : Policy Comparisons

Item	1980 Base Position	1980 Price Package	Price Harmonisation	Community Self-Sufficiency	Free Market
Self-supply (index):	130	125	128	124	88
Real price change (%)	0.0	-4.7	-1.8	-14.8	-34.6
FEOGA Budgetary Flows (mEUA):					
- gross expenditure	499	446	458	368	0
- income	-292	-346	-342	-211	0
- net expenditure	206	100	116	157	0
- VAT contribution	391	287	333	123	0
Balance and Effects (mEUA):					
- of FEOGA payments	-185	-187	-217	33	0
- of trade	684	607	691	492	-256
- of agric. payments	499	420	474	525	-256
- preferential trade effect	333	301	357	269	0
- budget and trade effect	148	114	140	302	0
Welfare Effect of Policy Changes (mEUA):					
- producers	0	-159	-61	-543	-1166
- consumers	0	109	46	339	1034
- taxpayers	0	104	59	268	391
- overall	0	55	44	64	260

Table 8.6 : United Kingdom : Policy Comparisons

Item	1980 Base Position	1980 Price Package	Price Harmonisation	Community Self-Sufficiency	Free Market
Self-supply (index):	86	83	84	75	68
Real price change (%):	0.0	-4.3	-3.3	-15.9	-30.4
FEOGA Budgetary Flows (mEUA):					
- gross expenditure	636	531	588	103	0
- income	-660	-708	-676	-423	0
- net expenditure	-24	-177	-89	-261	0
- VAT contribution	-1433	-1051	-1217	-452	0
Balances and Effects (mEUA):					
- of FEOGA payments	-1457	-1228	-1306	-712	0
- of trade	-1123	-1281	-1300	-2080	-2697
- of agric. payments	-2580	-2509	-2606	-2793	-2697
- pref. trade effect	-465	-424	-488	-148	-2697
- budget and trade effect	-1922	-1652	-1794	-860	0
Welfare Effect of Policy Changes (mEUA):					
- producers	0	-340	-267	-1255	-2484
- consumers	0	413	325	1540	3716
- taxpayers	0	382	216	981	1433
- overall	0	455	273	1266	2664

On its own, the 1980 price package did little
to alter this situation. Without it, the net FEOGA
position would have worsened, but the overall balance of agricultural payments remains almost unchanged. Farmers, however, would have been worse
off by 340 million EUA without the effects of a
series of green pound devaluations in the period up
to June 1980 (which raised nominal product prices to
UK farmers) and the strong rise of the UK pound
during 1980 against other currencies. These factors
led to the highest positive MCAs in the Community's
history, and in practice averted a deteriorating
situation. Due to the small positive MCAs used in
the present model (see Table 6.3), the harmonisation
policy has again a limited effect on the base situation. Community self-sufficiency in surplus products would substantially improve the UK's net
budgetary position, although producers would naturally suffer. Under free market conditions for the
EC, producers would be hardest hit, but the massive
potential gains to consumers as well as the equally
large gains to taxpayers do much to explain the
harkening-back in the UK towards the period in the
1950s and 1960s when a much higher degree of alignment with world prices was achieved.

IRELAND

The Republic of Ireland (Eire), with Denmark, was
brought into the Community in 1973 alongside the
United Kingdom, towards whom both the smaller countries had acted as traditional suppliers of agricultural products, and had other strong economic links
as members of the European Free Trade Association
(EFTA). From being strongly oriented towards the
United Kingdom in agricultural matters, Ireland has
found a new dimension in membership of the European
Community, and farming has reinforced its already
strong position within the Irish economy.
     Table 8.7 shows that Ireland is a major net
recipient of FEOGA expenditure, the small size of
the country being reflected in its small financial
contribution towards the Community's agricultural
budget. A highly positive balance of agricultural
trade and the large benefits the country receives
through high priced Community preference confirms
this impression.
     Without the 1980 price package, average Irish
prices would have been lower in real terms by nearly
four per cent, diminishing the financial advantages
somewhat, and the effect on producers leads to a
small overall loss in economic welfare. Price

Table 8.7 : Ireland : Policy Comparisons

Item	1980 Base Position	1980 Price Package	Price Harmonisation	Community Self-Sufficiency	Free Market
Self-supply (index):	307	299	310	245	226
Real price change (%):	0.0	-3.9	1.3	-17.7	-30.3
FEOGA Budgetary Flows (mEUA):					
- gross expenditure	644	564	651	81	0
- income	-21	-17	-22	-15	0
- net expenditure	623	547	629	66	0
- VAT contribution	71	52	60	22	0
Balances and Effects (mEUA):					
- of FEOGA payments	552	495	569	43	0
- of trade	1557	1506	1638	1476	969
- of agric. payments	2109	2001	2207	1519	969
- pref. trade effect	604	561	648	387	0
- budget and trade effect	1156	1056	1217	430	0
Welfare Effect of Policy Changes (mEUA):					
- producers	0	-89	31	-481	-693
- consumers	0	27	-13	96	230
- taxpayers	0	19	11	48	71
- overall	0	-43	29	-337	-392

harmonisation, on the other hand, would remove the negative Irish MCAs, and provide similar, if smaller, gains in these respects. Community self-sufficiency in surplus products bears particularly heavily on this country through its degree of dependence on milk products, while free market conditions would be even more deleterious, despite the gains to consumers.

DENMARK

In many ways, Denmark resembles Ireland in being a small country lacking any of the industrial centres of the European Community, and with an important agricultural sector geared to the export market. In Denmark's case, however, the farming balance is directed towards cereals and pigmeat (as opposed to Ireland's cattle and sheep), although both countries also rely on milk production. Table 8.8 shows a pattern very similar to that in Table 8.7 for Ireland; and there is little need to repeat the major points of interest. The small differences are mostly due to Denmark's lower rate of inflation and a somewhat different production pattern.

SYNTHESIS

While each of the previous sections has tried to outline the position of each member state of the European Community under five alternative states of agricultural policy, it is helpful in drawing conclusions to set the major policy effects for each country alongside each other, so that the balance of national gainers and losers can be more easily assessed.

Table 8.9 presents a set of results for two major measures of the impact which the CAP, and changes in it, have on the eight member-states included in the present analysis. The rows labelled 'A' show the balances of FEOGA payments: that is, gross expenditure under the CAP on agricultural guarantees and product or market support, less income from the agricultural levies and financial contributions arising in each country, the last item being adjusted for alternative policies according to the proportion of total VAT contributions found under the base position. For the Community as a whole, these balances naturally sum to zero. The rows labelled B give the overall welfare effect on producers, consumers and taxpayers of moving from the CAP in its base form to the specified alternatives (see Chapter 5 for further details).

Table 8.8 : Denmark : Policy Comparisons

Item	1980 Base Position	1980 Price Package	Price Harmonisation	Community Self-Sufficiency	Free Market
Self-supply (index):	237	230	237	213	168
Real price change (%):	0.0	-4.4	0.0	-16.6	-34.3
FEOGA Budgetary Flows (mEUA):					
- gross expenditure	1130	974	1080	560	0
- income	-33	-26	-33	-17	0
- net expenditure	1097	948	1047	544	0
- VAT contribution	217	159	184	68	0
Balance and Effects (mEUA):					
- of FEOGA payments	880	789	863	475	0
- of trade	1538	1439	1534	1055	671
- of agric. payments	2418	2229	2398	1530	671
- pref. trade effect	497	426	493	288	0
- budget and trade effect	1377	1215	1356	763	0
Welfare Effects of Policy Changes (mEUA):					
- producers	0	-157	0	-613	-1247
- consumers	0	47	0	115	456
- taxpayers	0	58	33	148	217
- overall	0	-53	33	-350	-575

Table 8.9 : Policy Comparisons by Country. (mEUA)

	EC9	Germany	France	Italy	Nether-lands	Belgium/ Luxembourg	United Kingdom	Ireland	Denmark
Base Position:									
A	0	-887	265	28	800	-185	-1457	552	880
B	0	0	0	0	0	0	0	0	0
1980 Price Package:									
A	0	-652	265	-306	819	-817	-1228	495	789
B	1894	789	367	331	-7	55	455	-43	-53
Price Harmonisation:									
A	0	-995	453	-105	732	-217	-1306	569	863
B	1407	575	307	135	11	44	273	29	33
Community Self-Sufficiency:									
A	0	-638	89	452	253	33	-712	43	475
B	3158	1757	491	727	-460	64	1266	-337	-350
Free Market:									
A	0	0	0	0	0	0	0	0	0
B	11051	5228	2213	2220	-566	260	2664	-392	-575

A = Net balance on FEOGA expenditure and financial contributions
B = Overall welfare effect (see text)

135

In the base position, the major net contribu-
tors are, as expected, Germany and the United Kingdom, with the Netherlands, Denmark and Ireland as
the main recipients. Without the 1980 price package,
the first two members enjoy reduced contributions
necessary to finance the lower level of production.
Italy finds itself a major contributor, while Ireland
has its net financial benefit somewhat reduced, as a
joint result of their balances of inflation and
product-mix. In overall welfare terms, absence of
the package hits Ireland and Denmark as countries
with high producer dependence on the CAP, but all
other members gain, particularly the paymasters
Germany and the United Kingdom. The Community as a
whole is estimated to have avoided the benefits of
almost 1900 million EUA through adoption of this
'prudent-pricing' package, in comparison with no
change in prices (i.e. no agreement).
    Harmonisation of prices to a common level equiv-
alent to the intervention price throughout the
Community from the base position of positive and
negative MCAs would increase the net financial
burden of Germany and Italy, to the (slight) benefit
of the Netherlands, the United Kingdom and Ireland.
In welfare terms, there is a gain to the Community
as a whole, mainly due to beneficial effects on
German consumers and taxpayers. There are no overall losers, although in the Benelux countries, producers losses outweigh consumer gains.
    Exact Community self-sufficiency in each product
in surplus in 1980 would be of major benefit to Italy
and the United Kingdom, though Germany finds its financial burden reduced, by almost a third. Ireland
and Denmark, currently dependent on the high prices
of surplus products, find that such a policy considerably reduces their gains. The overall welfare
effect of self-sufficiency in surplus products is not
as large for the Community as a whole as it is for
individual countries, since the larger net gains for
Germany, France, Italy and the United Kingdom are
offset by losses to the Netherlands, Ireland and
Denmark.
    A free market, by some definitions the ultimate
welfare optimum, (though here postulated only for
the EC and not other world trades) here records an
estimated 11000 million EUA advantage over the base
CAP position, with the major gainers being Germany
(5000 million EUA) and France, Italy and the United
Kingdom (over 2000 million EUA each). The Netherlands, Ireland and Denmark each lose over 400 million
EUA. This pattern is of interest in highlighting the
extreme protectionist stance of Germany, the roughly

equal position in welfare terms of France and United Kingdom, due at least in part to the relatively low VAT contribution by the latter country, and the substantial benefit which the CAP represents to most of the smaller members of the Community.

In conclusion, it should be noted that this chapter has dealt with the country-by-country impacts of specified policies and policy changes, as measured by a few financial and economic variables. For the purposes of carrying out the analysis, other factors, such as technical changes in production and temporal shifts in consumption, and other measures, such as the effects on farming structure, incomes and rents, have had to be ignored. In a full appraisal of the CAP by any particular nation, these factors and measures should of course be included, as they have been in the negotiating stances in the Council of Ministers. The present study has more limited aims, but the partial economic results offered in the tables of this chapter form an important contribution to more wide-ranging debates.

NOTES

1. An exploration of some of the economic and agricultural issues raised by enlargement of the EC to include Greece, Portugal and Spain is available in J.M.C. Rollo's 'The Second Enlargement of the European Economic Community : Some Economic Implications with Special Reference to Agriculture', Journal of Agricultural Economics, Vol. 30(3), 1979, pp.333-444.
2. The UK's base-level VAT contribution is calculated on the basis of the new financial agreement agreed at the June 1980 summit meeting at Venice, under which the UK's share of marginal expenditure was effectively reduced from 17.4 to about 12 per cent. However the complexities of the formulae included in the agreement as to the UK's share of expenditures above or below the base level have been ignored, as they were not designed to deal with the policy changes simulated in the present study. Instead, a strictly proportional approach has been adopted.

Chapter 9

DISTRIBUTIONAL EFFECTS AND POLICY EFFICIENCY

In a variety of ways, the previous three chapters
have reported the results of simulating the financial and economic effects of the CAP and some alternative policies applied to the agriculture of the EC.
The first part of this chapter illustrates some ways
in which such results can be used to provide deeper
insights into the distributional effects of policy
changes, by analysing the likely impact of policy
moves on different sections of the population, and
on farms of different sizes. Such an analysis
recognises the social and political importance of
distinguishing between groups affected in different
ways according to the nature of their dependence on
agriculture. The second part of the chapter concerns the use of the CAP market/budget model to
analyse the 'efficiency' of various shifts in policy
away from the base position.

DISTRIBUTIONAL EFFECTS OF THE CAP

Much of the continuous debate and negotiations
attaching to the development of the CAP cannot be
understood without an appreciation of the different
impacts which the policy, and changes within it,
have on various sections of society within each of
its member states. Individuals and their political
representatives would be expected to view an economic policy in rough proportion to the effects it
has on their own levels of real income or expenditures. An outline impression of these distributional effects can be gained by expressing them on a per
head basis for each of the major groups affected -
producers, users (or consumers), and taxpayers -
while recognising that a more refined analysis might
try to allow for both the interlocking membership of
these groups and their different relative levels of
income and wealth.

On the recipient side of the policy, the number employed in agriculture, forestry and fisheries (including self-employed farmers) in each member-state of the Community was taken as an indicator of those groups directly affected by the CAP through price guarantees and protective measures. In Table 9.1, the aggregate change in economic welfare of these groups for each of the policy changes described in Chapter 6 is expressed on a per capita basis. The lower half of the same table shows an equivalent analysis carried out for the changes in user and taxpayer welfare combined, using total working population as the appropriate denominator in these calculations.

The most striking, if not unexpected, aspect of the results in Table 9.1 is that producers are affected to a much greater extent than those who consume their output and finance the public expenditure involved. The difference far exceeds that which would reflect the proportion (about 25 per cent) of total consumer expenditure spent on agricultural products (including imports), and goes a long way towards explaining the resistance that has been observed towards many of the policies simulated in the present analysis. As between countries, the generally higher effects for producers in the northern countries compares with the low figures for Italy, while the user/taxpayer effects, though more uniform, show up the United Kingdom as generally the least affected of the member states, with Germany at the other end of the scale.

Farm Size Distribution

A more detailed analysis of the effect of the given policy changes on producers is achieved by apportioning the total changes in producers' welfare according to the size of farm businesses in each member state. A simple classification of farm businesses was carried out on the basis of the European size unit (ESU). Three sizes of farms were distinguished, and Table 9.2 shows their distribution within the Community as a whole.

The corresponding figures for producers in each member state (Table 9.3) emphasise the great variability of farming structure within the Community. For example, over 20 per cent of agricultural output in Italy is produced on small farms, while for all other countries except Eire the figure is less than 4 per cent. On the other hand, medium-sized farms produce between 7 per cent (Netherlands) and 40 per cent (Eire) of national output totals. A further

Table 9.1 : Policy Comparisons: Welfare Changes Per Head

	Germany	France	Italy	Nether-lands	Belg/Lux	U.K.	Eire	Denmark	EC9
Agricultural Employment ('000)	1544	1867	3012	279	128	632	220	208	7890
Producer Welfare Losses:				EUA/hd.					
- 1980 package	486	401	123	950	1241	539	404	757	365
- no MCAs	1094	0	0	416	477	422	-143	0	266
- self sufficiency	1649	1281	255	4038	4245	1986	2188	2947	1233
- free market	4207	2784	844	7932	9106	3931	3151	5997	2793
Total Employment ('000)	25017	21100	20287	4617	3910	24711	1049	2501	103192
User and Taxpayer Welfare Gains :				EUA/hd.					
- 1980 package	62	53	35	56	55	32	44	42	46
- no MCAs	91	15	7	27	27	22	-2	13	34
- self sufficiency	172	137	74	144	155	102	138	105	125
- free market	469	351	235	357	365	208	287	269	321

SOURCE : EC Commission, Agricultural Situation in the Community, 1980 Report, Table 71, and authors' estimates.

141

Table 9.2 : Farm Size Classification

| Type | ESUs[a] | Farms | Percentage of EC Total | | |
			UAA[b]	AWU[c]	UAA/AWU
Small	under 2	44	9	30	3
Medium	2 - 8	31	24	32	8
Large	over 8	25	67	38	20

SOURCE : EC Commission, Agricultural Situation in the Community, 1980 Report, Table 82.

NOTES:

a   European size unit. 1 ESU = 1000 ECU (about £530) of standard gross margin, corresponding to the returns from about 3 ha of wheat.

b   Utilisable agricultural area (ha).

c   Annual work unit (man-equivalent).

source of heterogeneity lies in differing manpower
levels between farms, even those of equivalent ESU
size. Taking 1 AWU as the standard level for small
farms (an overestimate of actual labour input but
not perhaps of income dependence), crude estimates
of AWU levels per farm in other size groups varied
up to 3.3 AWU per large farm in Italy and the United
Kingdom.[1] Table 9.3 gives the full set of such
estimates, and the changes in producer welfare for
two of the specified policies - the attainment of
exact self-sufficiency in products in surplus under
CAP in 1980, and a move to a free-market posture by
the EC in agricultural production, consumption and
trade, assuming, inter alia, that all farms share in
the necessary adjustments in proportion to their
original share of production.

The results indicate the approximate magnitude
of the economic task of compensating the various
farming groups for the burdens that would be imposed
upon them by these admittedly large policy moves.
For example, except in Italy (where special problems
of structure and production patterns exist), small
farmers in each member-state could be fully compensated for having to contribute towards the elimination of Community surpluses by sums under 100 mEUA.
At the other extreme, nearly 500 mEUA would be required to compensate large German farmers for having
to compete on a world market for their CAP products.
Naturally, the desirability of such compensation
and of the means of financing it are politically
sensitive issues. As an illustration of the possibilities, the taxpayer savings of moves to the
self-sufficiency and free-market policies were estimated in Chapter 6 at 5652 mEUA and 8255 mEUA
respectively. Thus, in principle, these sums would
be available to fund compensation without altering
the fiscal position of the Community. On this basis
the elimination of surpluses can be achieved at
fairly high levels of compensation to all farmers,
while free market conditions would involve considerable sacrifice to at least some producer groups.
The permutations of other possible schemes are
almost endless.

Impacts Per Farm and Per Worker

A final stage in this distributional analysis involves the calculation of the welfare impacts at the
level of the farm and the individual agricultural
worker. More precisely, the aggregate producer-
welfare effects at the foot of Table 9.3 may be
divided by the number of farms in each category,

Table 9.3 : Production, Labour Use and Producer Welfare Change, by Farm Size and Category

	Germany	France	Italy	Nether-lands	Belg/Lux	U.K.	Eire	Denmark	EC9
Proportion of Agric. Production (%):									
Small	3.1	2.8	21.0	0.3	2.9	2.0	10.1	0.9	6.4
Medium	20.1	17.6	35.1	6.6	13.5	11.9	40.6	13.4	20.5
Large	76.8	79.4	43.9	93.1	83.6	86.1	49.3	85.6	73.1
AWUs per Farm:									
Small	1.0	1.0	1.0	1.0	1.0	1.0	1.0	1.0	1.0
Medium	1.0	1.6	1.4	1.0	1.0	1.5	1.4	1.0	1.5
Large	2.1	2.2	3.3	1.7	1.6	3.3	2.3	1.6	2.3
Losses in Producer Welfare (mEUA) in Move from CAP 1980 to:									
1) EC Self-sufficiency									
Small	79	67	161	3	16	25	49	6	406
Medium	512	421	270	74	73	149	195	82	1777
Large	1956	1899	337	1049	454	1080	237	525	7537
2) Free Market									
Small	201	146	534	7	34	50	70	11	1052
Medium	1306	915	892	146	157	296	281	167	4160
Large	4989	4127	1116	2060	974	2139	342	1068	16815

SOURCE : Authors' estimates

and again by the average number of workers on each farm, for each member state. The results are shown in Table 9.4.

The results in the upper half of the table indicate the magnitude of the direct losses on farms of different sizes if either of the two policies of surplus elimination or free markets were followed. As a rough guide, these figures may be compared with the total standard gross margins of each category, i.e. small, under 2000 EUA; medium, 2000-8000 EUA; and large, over 8000 EUA. Of course, the gross effect of such massive changes in policy would in practice be partly passed on to the suppliers of such inputs as land, hired labour, variable inputs and capital goods, through lower rents, wages and prices. Nevertheless, the impacts are high for both policy moves, and indicate the very serious magnitude of the impact on all three sizes of farm.

The lower half of Table 9.4 adjusts the previous figures for the estimated number of persons working on each farm (see Table 9.3). For comparison with these effects, which range from 100 to 10,000 EUA per AWU, the average net value-added in EC agriculture at factor cost is about 6000 EUA per AWU. Even allowing for the higher productivity of their workers, the larger farms seem particularly vulnerable to policy changes of the types modelled, often suffering a per capita loss of some ten times that on small farms in the same country.

It will be clear that the above analysis is open to a considerable degree of refinement. Apart from the problems mentioned above of differing price-responsiveness between farms of different sizes, no account has been taken of production patterns below the level of the nation-state, and a regional analysis of the distributional effect of changes in the CAP seems particularly worthwhile.[2] It should be relatively easy to improve the labour utilisation figures, and thus the estimates of gross impact per agricultural worker, but there remains the more difficult task of allowing for part-time agricultural workers of various types. A further complex, but potentially rewarding, avenue of inquiry concerns the secondary impacts on factor markets other than hired labour.

Table 9.4 : Producer Welfare Effects, by Farm and by worker, by Farm Size Category

(EUA)

	Germany	France	Italy	Nether-lands	Belg/Lux.	U.K.	Eire	Denmark	EC9
Producer Losses Per Farm in Move from CAP 1980 to:									
1) EC Self-Sufficiency									
Small	321	191	92	393	372	372	476	380	157
Medium	1503	928	376	1854	1798	1709	2048	1786	976
Large	6084	3713	1757	9177	7472	8630	7755	7349	5275
2) Free Market									
Small	818	416	304	772	797	736	686	774	407
Medium	3835	2016	1245	3642	3857	3382	2950	3634	2285
Large	15522	8068	5819	18025	16027	17083	11169	14954	11767
Losses Per AWU in Move from CAP 1980 to:									
1) EC Self-Sufficiency									
Small	321	191	92	393	372	372	476	380	157
Medium	1503	580	269	1854	1798	1139	1403	1786	651
Large	2897	1688	533	5398	4670	2615	3372	4593	2293
2) Free Market									
Small	818	416	304	772	797	736	686	774	407
Medium	3835	1260	390	3642	3857	2255	2107	4634	1523
Large	7392	3667	1763	10603	10017	5177	4856	9346	5116

The second part of this chapter concerns the use of
the CAP market/budget model to analyse the
'efficiency' of various shifts in policy away from
the 1980 base level. Efficiency is used here in the
conventional economic sense of relating the marginal
(step-by-step) achievement of desired goals to the
costs of doing so. Whereas in the case of the
single-firm, the input-output relationship is
usually clear in principle, if difficult to model
mathematically, the application of efficiency
analysis to policy objectives and costs opens up a
wide area of controversy as to the proper definition
and measurement of both output (objectives) and
input (policy resources). While not wishing to deny
the importance of such debate, it seems more fruit-
ful in the present context to limit the possibilities to a few variables most closely associated with
the current CAP situation. Variables such as aggregate producer incomes and FEOGA expenditure link
directly to the level of price support offered under
the CAP, but do not attempt to span the wide range
of social and political factors which perhaps should
be taken into account in a full analysis of agricultural policies. The present analysis is thus limited to the 'internal' efficiency of the CAP as a
set of price support arrangements which can be
altered in various ways, rather than encompassing
the wider comparison of the CAP with alternative
policies such as deficiency payments or direct income support, which would determine the 'external'
efficiency of the CAP as a suitable type of agricultural policy.
     Following Josling,[4] the upper half of Figure
9.1 shows relationships between total 'cost' and
'effect', for any particular choice of these two
concepts, and for specific ranges of policy options.
The point P represents the base position of the CAP
as modelled in 1980, from which policy moves may be
made to increase (or decrease) the desired effect,
normally at higher (or lower) cost. For any specified set of policy changes (e.g. uniform percentage
price increases or decreases on all CAP products, or
moves towards or away from some desired set of price
levels different from the current set) curves such
as AB and CD trace out available alternative positions to P. The cost-effectiveness of such moves is
given by the slope of such curves, which may be expected to show falling marginal returns (increasing
costs)[5] as shown in the lower half of Figure 9.1.
Larger shifts of policy may give rise to different

FIGURE 9.1 COST-EFFECT ANALYSIS OF POLICY ALTERNATIVES

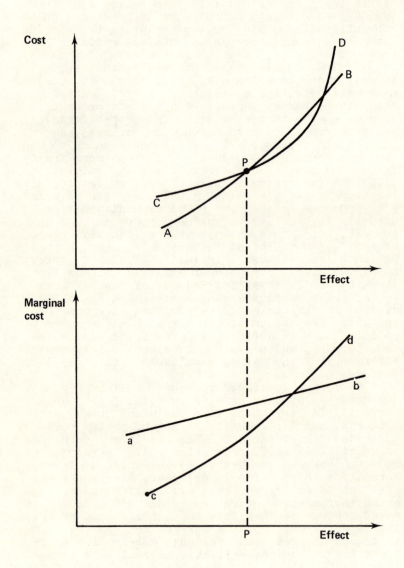

cost/effect rankings, as shown by the crossing of curves AB and CD to the right of P. Similar diagrams of cost-effect curves can of course be constructed not only for other types of policy shift away from CAP 1980 but for different definitions and combinations of cost and effect measures.

The present analysis takes as suitable measures of policy effects:

1) real farm incomes, as approximated by the EUA changes in producer welfare;

2) an index of farm prices; and

3) an index of self-supply.

These correspond to three of the five Article 39.1 objectives of the CAP (see Chapter 2) - i.e. improvement in agricultural earnings, 'reasonable' prices, and assured supplies of food. As 'costs', four measures already introduced in Chapter 5 are used:

a) gross FEOGA expenditure;

b) taxation, to finance the policy in question;

c) user costs, i.e. changes in user and consumer economic welfare;

d) resource costs, i.e. changes in overall economic welfare, as measured by the net sum of producer, consumer and taxpayer effects.

The costs, in terms of (a) to (d) above of achieving a unit 'gain' in each of the effects (1) to (3) above, have been calculated for a number of policy changes, viz:

i) percentage changes in administered price levels applied uniformly to all commodities and all member-states;

ii) elimination of the MCAs applying in 1980;

iii) moves towards or away from exact self-sufficiency in such commodity in surplus; and

iv) moves towards or away from a completely free market attitude by the EC towards agricultural commodities.

EFFICIENCY RESULTS

The costs per unit effect achieved through each of
these policy alternatives will vary according to the
extent of the change involved, and hence for policy
changes (i),(iii) and (iv), both full and 'partial'[6]
versions were run. For example, once the price
changes consequent on a complete adoption by the
Community of a free market policy stance have been
calculated, it is possible, and no doubt more realistic, to examine the effects of the same pattern of
changes, but at much smaller magnitudes, which might
be taken to represent a move towards less protected
markets (or, with signs reversed, an increase in
protection).
     The effects of the four types of policy move
are illustrated in Table 9.5, for both full and,
where applicable, 'partial' moves. Lower prices (in
real terms) reduce both farm incomes and the overall
self-supply index, but the extent of these reductions depends on the pattern of the price decreases.
A move to free markets, for example, reduces livestock product prices more than those of crops, whereas the elimination of surpluses has a less serious
impact on non-milk livestock products. The overall
effect of a complete move to free markets is a 30
per cent price fall, more than twice the 13 per cent
drop required to eliminate surpluses. Smaller,
partial policy moves of the same types are represented by the P and P' rows of the table, and can be
compared with arbitrary positive and negative across-
the-board changes of 10 per cent in price levels.
     To obtain efficiency or cost-effectiveness co-
efficients for these various policy moves, the
change in each cost is divided by the change in each
effect. For example, a uniform increase in real
prices of 10 per cent leads to an extra FEOGA expenditure cost of 6701 mEUA, while raising farm incomes
by 6570 mEUA. Hence the (average) efficiency of
such a move is 6701/6570 = 1.02 EUAs of FEOGA expenditure per unit EUA rise in farm incomes. As well as
such average coefficients corresponding to the full
and partial policy moves of Table 9.5, it is also
possible, by considering very small price changes, to
obtain marginal coefficients at the base position
for three of the four types of policy changes - the
exception being the elimination of MCAs, itself a
relatively small adjustment. The full set of efficiency coefficients are set out in Table 9.6, in
which, for example, the first column of figures
gives the cost in terms of gross expenditure under
FEOGA of achieving a 1 EUA rise in farm incomes, as

Table 9.5 : Effects of Policy Changes From CAP 1980

| | | Changes in: | | |
		Farm Incomes (mEUA)	Real Farm Prices (%)	Index of EC Self-Supply (%)
Alternative Policy:				
Uniform Price	-10%	-6325	-10.00	-8.9
Change	+10%	+6570	+10.00	+8.9
No MCAs	F	-1646	-2.21	-1.9
Self-Sufficiency	F	-8995	-13.28	-12.7
in EC Surplus	P	-1074	-1.85	-1.5
Products	P'	+1099	+1.96	+1.6
Free Market	F	-19144	-29.84	-28.3
	P	-2114	-3.28	-3.5
	P'	+2165	+3.32	+3.5

NOTE : F indicates a full move, and P (P') a partial move of 10% (-10%) of the price changes implied in F, towards the alternative policy specified.

Table 9.6 : Costs Per Unit Effect of Policy Changes From CAP 1980

(EC 9)

Effect:		Farm Incomes				Farm Prices				EC Self-Supply			
Cost[1]:		E	T	U	W	E	T	U	W	E	T	U	W
Alternative Policy[2]:		(EUA/EUA)				(mEUA/1% real price)				(mEUA/1% index change)			
Uniform price change	-10%	0.59	0.80	0.90	0.70	369	496	562	434	416	560	633	490
	M	0.76	0.91	0.86	0.77	487	579	550	488	553	657	624	554
	+10%	1.02	0.97	0.82	0.79	668	633	539	520	754	719	608	586
No MCAs	F	0.49	0.72	1.09	0.80	367	535	811	600	421	615	931	689
Self-Sufficiency in EC Surplus Products	F	0.79	0.67	0.72	0.39	535	454	489	266	559	474	512	278
	P	1.26	1.14	0.62	0.77	733	666	362	446	901	819	445	548
	M	1.30	1.18	0.61	0.80	743	680	348	457	921	842	431	565
	P'	1.33	1.22	0.60	0.82	746	687	335	461	932	859	419	576
Free Market	F	0.59	0.45	1.07	0.52	377	286	688	333	401	304	733	354
	P	0.70	1.04	0.87	0.91	450	696	582	611	450	672	560	588
	M	0.78	1.05	0.85	0.90	503	675	551	579	522	701	573	601
	P'	1.00	1.05	0.83	0.89	654	685	544	577	677	709	564	598

1. E indicates gross FEOGA expenditure; T taxation (VAT-based budgetary contributions); U user expenditure; and W overall economic welfare or resource cost.

2. M indicates a small (marginal) change from the base 1980 position in the direction indicated. F indicates a full move, and P (P') a partial move of 10% (-10%) of the price changes implied in F, towards the alternative policy specified. Costs against M are marginal costs; those against other sub-headings are average costs over the full or partial policy move.

measured by change in producer welfare. Equivalently, these figures give the saving in terms of gross expenditure achievable at the cost of a unit drop in farm incomes. Clearly, if the most pressing objective is to raise farm incomes, a low figure is desired. If the goal is reduction in expenditure, a high figure indicates an attractive policy option.

The figures in the table in the rows labelled F, P and P' are average efficiency measures. The pattern of F, P and P' coefficients for a given effect, cost and policy change reveals the expected increasing average costs of achieving a policy effect by increasing the level of support given. For example, for the free market policy moving from the base position to P and then F involves reduction in the degree of support, and the corresponding average cost in terms of FEOGA expenditure falls accordingly. Moving to P' in the other direction, further away from a free market, a higher average FEOGA cost of 1 EUA per cent of producer income is found. Given these average cost values, estimates may be made of the corresponding marginal costs within the same range of policy moves. The figures in the rows labelled M indicate the marginal costs at the base position. Comparisons of the marginal costs shows that uniform price changes are about as cost-effective as moves towards or away from free-market conditions (a 100 EUA rise in farm incomes involving a 77 EUA rise in gross FEOGA expenditure) while marginally altering the level of self-supply in surplus products involves considerably more expense to achieve the same end but offers the greatest savings for a given income drop. Full elimination of surpluses, however, reduces FEOGA expenditure by a roughly similar amount per unit decrease in farm incomes to the marginal price-level and free-market moves described above. Figure 9.2 shows marginal cost curves derived from the first columns of Tables 9.5 and 9.6. (The marginal costs at non-zero levels of farm income change have been calculated by rough extrapolation from the partial and average costs in the P and F rows of Table 9.6). The steepening costs of moving away from free-market price levels are obvious in the figure, and threaten to overtake the marginal costs of increasing EC self-supply in surplus products, although the latter are higher at the base position. Similar graphs can be constructed for each of the twelve columns of Table 9.6.

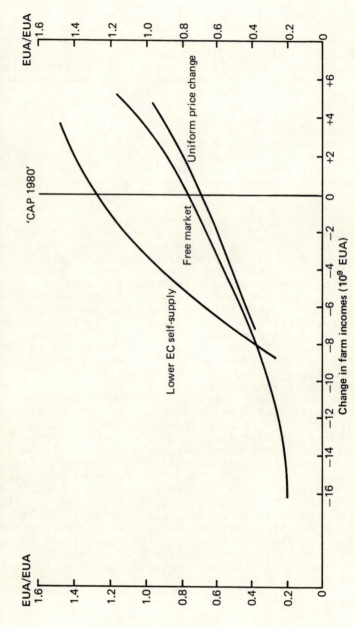

FIGURE 9.2 MARGINAL CHANGE IN GROSS FEOGA EXPENDITURE PER UNIT CHANGE IN FARM INCOMES

Comparing all four cost measures of efforts to raise (or lower) farm incomes by the specified policy moves, marginal uniform price changes incur lower tax increases and welfare losses than the other two types of marginal policy moves. However, the costs in terms of increases in expenditure by users of the agricultural commodities (other than farmers themselves), which decrease with higher levels of protection under CAP as consumers reduce demand, are heavier when all prices are equally affected rather than being concentrated on products in surplus or priced far from free-market levels. In summary, therefore, it appears that it is more 'efficient' to raise farm incomes by across-the-board price increases from all points of view except that of consumers, rather than to adopt any of the other policy price patterns considered here. Conversely, for a given acceptable lowering in farm incomes, the reduction of surpluses promises the largest fiscal benefits, although freer markets generally offer rather better overall economic gains.

In terms of the other objectives considered in Table 9.6 - farm price levels and overall Community self-supply - somewhat similar interpretations can be made. For example, the budgetary saving in lowering the level of farm prices by an average 1 per cent in real terms is somewhat under 500 million EUA if this is done through uniform price decreases or by moves towards free-market price levels, but about 750 million EUA if price cuts are concentrated on products already in surplus. To achieve a 1 per cent rise in the self-supply index would require extra FEOGA expenditure of 500-550 million EUA through the first two types of price increases, compared to 920 million EUA extra spent on products already in surplus.

Few realistic analyses of the CAP can avoid discussion of policy options from the point of view of the member states themselves as opposed to that of the Community as a whole. In the present context, therefore, the efficiency measures of Table 9.6 are re-calculated at national level, taking into account the differing conditions of production and consumption of agricultural products, the different price levels brought about by the use of green rates, and each country's VAT-based financial contribution to the Community budget as agreed in June 1980. Table 9.7 presents such figures for the marginal costs of raising farm incomes through the three main types of policy change so far analysed. Full discussion would again be somewhat tedious, but the general situations of different member states are worth

Table 9.7 : Marginal Costs of Raising Farm Incomes, by Country

(EUA/EUA)

Cost	Policy Measures[1]	G	F	I	N	Be/L	UK	Ir	Dk	EC9
Gross FEOGA Expenditure	P	0.61	0.64	0.74	1.25	0.44	0.32	2.15	1.76	0.76
	SS	1.26	1.13	1.69	1.62	0.91	0.77	2.31	2.19	1.30
	FM	0.70	0.48	0.58	1.21	0.43	0.25	1.70	2.12	0.78
Taxation	P	1.19	0.90	0.84	0.62	0.95	0.89	0.23	0.49	0.91
	SS	1.44	1.23	2.50	0.70	1.24	1.09	0.21	0.54	1.18
	FM	1.30	1.10	1.11	0.64	1.08	1.10	0.25	0.52	1.05
User Expenditure	P	1.02	0.74	1.19	0.44	0.80	1.17	0.26	0.29	0.85
	SS	0.77	0.48	1.19	0.23	0.60	0.96	0.16	0.18	0.61
	FM	1.00	0.77	1.26	0.39	0.79	1.19	0.24	0.28	0.85
Overall Expenditure	P	1.22	0.63	1.03	0.06	0.75	1.06	-0.50	-0.21	0.76
	SS	1.20	0.71	2.70	-0.07	0.84	1.06	-0.62	-0.27	0.80
	FM	1.30	0.87	1.37	-0.03	0.87	1.30	-0.50	-0.20	0.90

1. P represents uniform price increases; SS, a move towards 100% EC self-sufficiency in surplus products; and FM a move towards free market conditions, by the EC.

noting. German taxpayers and consumers clearly pay
a relatively heavy price for all three types of
policy move (and would conversely benefit more if
farm incomes could be lowered), while France would
be much less burdened by higher prices, even those
involving further departures from free markets.
Italian taxpayers and users are particularly hard-
hit by the surpluses financed under the CAP. The
incomes of farmers in the Netherlands, Ireland and
Denmark - all countries with important agricultural
sectors heavily dependent on exported products - can
only be raised through substantial increases in
FEOGA expenditures in those countries, but the overall economic impact on these countries is usually
beneficial, as evidenced by negative cost coefficients. Belgium/Luxembourg occupies an unobtrus-
ively average position on most counts. The United
Kingdom exhibits the expected low marginal FEOGA expenditure costs, but the costs to users of agricultural products are high. However, the re-formulated
UK contributions to the financing of the CAP reduce
her marginal taxation burden to average levels.
     As an illustration of how the efficiency of
policy moves within the CAP framework can be measured
within the distributional framework explained in the
first part of this chapter, Table 9.8 contains some
preliminary estimates of the effect on the incomes
of agricultural workers on farms of various sizes,
in each member state and for three policy changes.
It is noticeable how countries with a low labour
intensity on large farms (such as the Netherlands)
are vulnerable under all these changes in policy,
while agricultural workers in France suffer less in
absolute losses. The Italian figures are lower
still, but this may be partly caused by a bias in
product coverage of the model.

DISCUSSION

The results presented in Tables 9.6 and 9.7 above
allow a deceptively simple answer to the question of
the efficiency of CAP. At the margin, the policy is
56 per cent efficient! That is, taxpayers and consumers collectively give up 1.77 EUA for the marginal EUA transferred to producers through a uniform
percentage increase in the major CAP commodity
prices. Different price changes (increasing self-
supply or increasing protection) are shown to be
less efficient in this sense as ways of improving
farm incomes (55 per cent and 52 per cent respectively). Equivalent calculations for each member
state for a uniform price change produce the

Table 9.8 : Effects of Policy Change from CAP 1980 on Agricultural Worker Incomes, by Country and Farm Size Category

(EUA/annual work unit)

Alternative Policy	Farm Size Group (ESU)	Country								
		G	F	I	N	Be/L	UK	Ir	Dk	EC9
5% fall in real farm prices	Under 2	105	70	50	105	100	115	110	100	80
	2-8	495	205	140	495	490	355	355	475	240
	Over 8	900	595	280	1440	1265	790	810	1220	710
	All	540	450	135	1080	1150	510	615	780	405
Elimination of EC surpluses	Under 2	295	179	82	367	320	466	353	341	223
	2-8	1381	543	239	1733	1546	1432	1083	1601	675
	Over 8	2661	1579	474	5046	4015	3299	2486	4119	2001
	All	1515	1199	227	3775	3650	2141	1887	2643	1140
Free Market	Under 2	740	360	245	672	607	665	665	631	474
	2-8	3469	1092	716	3169	2936	2037	2037	1959	1437
	Over 8	6686	3178	1420	9224	7624	4676	4676	7612	4258
	All	3806	2412	680	6900	6931	3550	3550	4884	2426

NOTE : Aggregate income changes estimated by authors, distributed between farm sizes on the basis of total agricultural output distribution implied by productivity rates and farm size distributions (see Agricultural Situation in the Community, 1980, European Commission, Tables 69 and 82). This distribution of output (and average annual work unit per farm) is based on 1975 data.

following values: Germany: 45 per cent; UK: 48 per
cent; Italy: 49 per cent; Belgium and Luxembourg: 56
per cent; France: 60 per cent; Netherlands: 93 per
cent; Denmark: 102 per cent; and Ireland: 105 per
cent. The converse of these results is, of course,
that taxpayers and consumers together can gain from
1.77 EUA to 1.90 EUA (uniform price reduction and
price reduction towards free markets respectively)
for a 1 EUA reduction in producer incomes.

The current CAP problem is most frequently cast
as budgetary/surplus problem, and it can be seen
that reductions in prices for those commodities in
surplus are highly efficient in terms of maximum
benefit (saving) to taxpayers and FEOGA expenditure
per unit loss to producers. Benefits of such a
policy change to consumers, however, are more limited than would be provided by a move towards free
markets. Formal analysis and complex model building
may seem hardly necessary to derive these conclusions, but the quantitative estimates of the effects
are illuminating. For example, the economic welfare
effects of changes in farm prices (Table 9.6) are
estimated here as not inconsiderable, being of comparable size to the effects on gross FEOGA expenditure (except when price changes are restricted to
those commodities in surplus). As estimates of
market-diagram triangles, or deadweight resource
costs, 450-500 million EUA loss per 1 per cent
price increase is, perhaps, surprisingly large in
comparison with the losses generated under more
partial analysis. These costs are also associated,
of course, with increases in Community self-supply
and serve as a strong counter-argument to the politically attractive goal of self-sufficiency.

The empirical results presented here are
limited, but the methodological framework clearly
allows for the comparison of other income support
policies with the current price support system in
terms of their overall efficiency as well as in
terms of taxpayer and consumer efficiency. To recall a distinction made earlier, the present empirical analysis refers to the internal efficiency of
the CAP, that is, the impact of changing the settings
of certain policy instruments of the CAP (mainly
prices) in certain defined ways. The external
efficiency - whether other types of agricultural
policy would achieve similar ends more effectively -
remains to be examined, but given adequate specification of such alternatives to CAP, comparable estimates could be produced within the framework used in
this study.

Such answers, however, leave a multitude of
questions unanswered. Are there other policies (deficiency payments, direct income payments, etc.)
which are more efficient in transferring income to
producers? To what extent is the transfer of income
to producers possible in any event given the competition for limited agricultural resources and the
possible lack of competition in the input supply
industries? To which producers and which regions is
it desirable to try and transfer income? To what
extent is the current distribution of the burden of
transfers between consumers and taxpayer (and thus
between countries) efficient, that is, would an
alternative distribution save economic resources and
increase total incomes?
     Questions about the desirability and effective-
ness of income transfers have been excluded from
efficiency questions per se in the approach adopted
here. In exactly analogous fashion with the usual
economic analysis of market efficiency, the establishment of an optimally efficient policy requires
the specification not only of an objective function
but a set of available options amongst which choice
is possible. Such specifications, in the context of
so complex and wide-ranging a policy as the CAP, are
hard to agree, since they involve not only perennial
questions of the weights to be given to the impacts
of change on different groups of people, but also a
consensus, albeit temporary, on the nature and political acceptability of alternative policies. In
this situation, the provision of relevant measures
of the cost-effectiveness of certain policy changes,
as attempted in this chapter, may not provide any
final answers to the question of CAP efficiency, but
it does represent a necessary element of the debate.

NOTES

1.   The data source for these estimates is EC
Commission, Agricultural Situation in the Community,
1980 Report, Tables 69 and 82.
2.   See, for example, Regional Impact of the Common
Agricultural Policy: Italian Report, University of
Naples, November 1980, for an interesting analysis
of value-added in the regional agricultures of Italy.
3.   This section is a shorter version of K.J.
Thomson and D.R. Harvey, 'The Efficiency of the
Common Agricultural Policy', to appear in European
Review of Agricultural Economics, 1982.
4.   See Josling, T.E. 'Agricultural Policies in Developed Countries: A Review', Journal of Agricultural Economics, Vol. 25 (3), Sept.1974,pp.229-263.

5.   See Appendix I of the paper referred to in Note 3 above for a mathematical analysis of this point.
6.   The term 'partial' is used here to distinguish a relatively large policy change from one that would correspond to a move to or from the origin of Figure 9.1, to the point in question, i.e. the 'average' cost as used in the theory of the firm. The precise definition of 'origin' in the policy context is both debatable and of limited practical importance.

Chapter 10

CONCLUSIONS

THE ANALYTIC FRAMEWORK

The European Community's Common Agricultural Policy
has given rise to various financial and economic
flows between the member states and between the producers, consumers and taxpayers of the Community.
In order to analyse and estimate these transfers it
has been necessary to simplify the complexities of
the real CAP to a form amenable to coherent analysis
and computational modelling. The consequential but
unavoidable loss of some commodity- and country-
specific detail is the price to be paid for being
able to adopt a Community-wide viewpoint towards the
analysis of the CAP and the changes in policy which
are inherent in the concepts of costs and benefits
arising out of its operation.

The Commission of the European Communities has
characterised the CAP "as a system of support of
farmers' incomes mainly through the support of
market prices"[1]. In terms of the objectives set out
for the CAP in the Treaty of Rome, this emphasis on
the income support role of the policy relegates all
other objectives to subsidiary roles. It is true
that, in the Treaty, ensuring reasonable prices to
consumers, and increasing agricultural productivity,
are given as additional objectives. But if farm incomes are the central focus of the policy then the
implication is that these objectives should be pursued only insofar as they contribute to, or at least
do not conflict with, the primary objective of income support.

The policy of price support, through variable
import levies, export subsidies and intervention
purchases, inevitably results in transfers of income
from consumers or users of agricultural output to
producers. To the extent that budgetary revenues
arising from the CAP (import and other levies) are

163

not sufficient to cover expenditure generated by the policy (export subsidies and the cost of intervention purchases), the policy will also result in transfers from taxpayers to producers. The CAP, as a supra-national policy, also includes the elements of common financing and Community preference. Many of these transfers from consumers and taxpayers to producers will take place across national frontiers, from one member country to another. It is these transfers which give rise to the various notions of the costs(and benefits) of the CAP.

Chapters 3 and 5 describe in detail the components of CAP-related transfers. Three principal categories of cost (or benefit) to each member state are identified: (i) net transactions with FEOGA, the agricultural part of the EC expenditure budget; (ii) the net balance of payments on agricultural transactions combining the balance of agricultural trade and the general (VAT) budgetary contribution; and (iii) economic welfare costs to producers, consumers, taxpayers and for the member-state as a whole. Categories (i) and (ii) may be considered either in terms of the total net flow resulting from a particular policy or in terms of the changes in the flow consequent on a change from one policy (the present CAP) to another. The category (iii) welfare effects are described only as the welfare changes resulting from a change in policy. Any discussion of the 'cost of the CAP' must first, therefore, specify which of the above aspects are of interest.

To further complicate the picture, it will be clear by now that the level of any specific category of cost will depend also on the base and alternative policies assumed. In this study four alternatives to the CAP as it existed in 1979/80 have been considered ranging from the politically feasible set of measures introduced in the 1980 price package to the unlikely, but economically interesting, case of a free market between the Community and her trading partners.

The results of these analyses confirm the generally held view that the transfers arising from the support levels of the CAP are regressive within member countries and inequitable between them. The first inequitable characteristic of the common price support mechanism arises from the facts that the policy does not include all agricultural commodities (potatoes, and, until recently, sheepmeat, being notable exceptions) and that not all included commodities are equally supported. In particular, the degree of support provided for mediterranean products (wine, olive oil and horticultural products) is generally less than the level of support provided for the northern temperate products. Even within the latter, the degree of nominal protection (measured as the difference between Community and world price levels) varies considerably between products and also over time[2]. The two major consequences of this characteristic are that the transfers between consumers, taxpayers, producers and countries will depend on the different production and consumption mixtures of commodities (favouring some countries and regions at the expense of others) and will also vary through time as the level of protection varies. Chapter 7 contains a commodity-by-commodity analysis of the costs and benefits of the CAP and alternative policies.

Secondly, the inequities between member countries arise because the operation of CAP causes a transfer of income from those countries (and regions) which are less than self-sufficient in the agricultural commodities covered by the CAP (that is, those countries which are larger consumers than producers) to those countries which are more than self-sufficient. Figures showing such transfers are described in detail in Chapter 8. The transfers occur through the EC budget via import levies, export subsidies, and VAT contributions needed to finance the policy, and also directly from consumers in the importing countries to producers in the exporting countries as a result of Community preference, that is trading at Community-supported prices. Such transfers are inevitable consequences of a common policy to support agricultural prices, but they will only accidentally result in progressive transfers from richer to poorer countries.[3] Of course, there is no reason to expect a single policy such as the CAP to result in progressive or convergent inter-country transfers in and of itself. However, the dominant and almost overpowering position of the CAP within the spectrum of European policies is bound to make this accidental feature of the policy a prominent issue in member state concerns about the Community and its future development, as illustrated by the United Kingdom's complaints over net budgetary contributions in 1979 and 1980.

Thirdly, food consumption expenditure generally accounts for a larger proportion of total expenditure or disposable income for poorer people than for the richer members of society. Producers, on the other hand, benefit from the policy in proportion to their total production, so that the larger and richer farmers will tend to receive a greater share of the benefits. The result is that the transfer from consumers to producers is regressive, that is in greater proportion from the poor and in greater proportion to the rich. Chapter 9 contains a preliminary analysis of this aspect of the CAP as regards the distributional impact on producers, but clearly more remains to be done.

THE ESTIMATED COSTS OF THE CAP

Given that the CAP actually supports agricultural prices at a higher level than would otherwise be the case, the general direction of the resulting transfers from consumers, taxpayers and importing or less than self-sufficient countries, to producers and exporting countries is clear. However, quantification of these transfers requires that the extent to which prices are higher than they would otherwise be is also made explicit. In other words, the policy alternative must be spelt out.

Recently, the most widely discussed "costs of CAP" (in the United Kingdom at least) have been premised on an alternative policy which involves maintaining current levels of price support but abandoning Community preference and common financing. Studies giving rise to those estimated costs are reviewed in Chapter 4. These studies concentrate on the inter-country or "across-the-exchanges" transfers generated by the common elements of the policy to the exclusion of all other transfers. Such transfers do not have any paramount claim to being the costs of the CAP. Even their relevance is questionable as few significant groups in Europe are calling for the alternative policy on which they are based. The assumption that price levels would be unchanged in a move from common to national policies makes computation of the transfers simpler, but is clearly very restrictive. It seems unlikely that the member states would be willing to maintain the same level of support for their agricultural industries under a national policy as they are under a common policy. In any event, such nationalisation is only one of a range of alternative policies which might be considered, and a relatively disagreeable option at that, at least to those member states committed to the European ideal. While the balance of payments transfers which stem from the common financing and Community preference principles of the CAP may be of some interest for some purposes, they represent an incomplete picture of the total transfers consequent upon the CAP as measured against specific alternatives.

166

A more complete, if still grossly aggregated, set of transfers is summarised as "The costs of the CAP" in Table 10.1. The size of the table and the volume of information in it is somewhat overwhelming, but it accurately reflects the wide range of figures which have some claim to being called the costs of the CAP. Four separate alternative policy options are examined. The effect of the 1980 price package adopted in the spring of that year can be assessed against the policy of prices unchanged from the previous year. Harmonisation of prices involves the elimination of monetary compensatory amounts (MCAs) as they existed in Early 1980. Community self-sufficiency represents a policy which reduces Community prices by the amount necessary to bring supplies of each commodity in surplus into balance with demand for the Community as a whole. A free market policy implies the dismantling of all of the current price support mechanisms of the CAP, and free trade at the resulting world price levels for all CAP commodities.

For each of these policy options, calculations have been performed by means of a computer policy simulation model (see Chapter 5) to estimate the physical, financial and economic consequences of moving from the 'base' position of the CAP as it operated in 1980 to the specified alternative, all other factors being held constant. A policy involving on average a fall in real prices, for example, would be expected to reduce production, increase consumption and result in a fall in Community expenditure on the disposal of surplus commodities. The pattern of these effects by country and commodity would depend, of course, on the particular combination of changes in prices and exchange rates which make up the move from the base position to the alternative. Correspondingly, the economic effects of such moves on producers, consumers and taxpayers are the result of a complex combination of these factors. The overall changes in economic welfare for these three groups in each member-state and the Community as a whole are reported in Table 10.1.[4]

The 1980 price package represented a fall in real support prices for most CAP commodities. However, in the inflationary conditions of that year, the absence of such an agreement, and the continuation of the previous year's price levels, would have resulted in an even steeper real price decline. The cost of this alternative against that of the CAP as it stood in 1980 is therefore measurable by the changes that would have taken place in the absence of the 1980 agreement. The results in Section 1 of

167

Table 10.1 : The Costs of the CAP
Changes in Economic Welfare, by Alternatives to CAP 1980 (mEUA)

	EC9 Total	Ger.	France	Italy	Neth.	Belg/Lux.	U.K.	Ire.	Den.
I: 1980 Price Package									
Producers	-2879	-750	-748	-370	-265	-159	-340	-89	-157
Consumers	2573	817	573	461	125	109	413	27	47
Taxpayers	2200	721	543	240	133	104	382	19	58
Net	1894	789	367	331	-7	55	455	-43	-53
II: Price Harmonisation									
Producers	-2102	-1690	0	0	-116	-61	-267	31	0
Consumers	2267	1857	0	0	51	46	325	-13	0
Taxpayers	1243	407	307	135	75	59	216	11	33
Net	1407	575	307	135	11	44	273	29	33
III: Community Self-Sufficiency									
Producers	-9725	-2546	-2392	-768	-1127	-543	-1255	-481	-613
Consumers	7231	2450	1488	879	324	339	1540	96	115
Taxpayers	5652	1854	1394	616	342	268	981	48	148
Net	3158	1757	491	727	-460	64	1266	-337	-350
IV: Free Market									
Producers	-22039	-6496	-5198	-2542	-2213	-1166	-2484	-693	-1247
Consumers	24836	9017	5374	3863	1147	1034	3716	230	456
Taxpayers	8255	2707	2037	900	500	391	1433	71	217
Net	11051	5228	2213	2220	-566	260	2664	-392	-575

SOURCE : Author's estimates.

Table 10.1 show a difference of nearly 3000 million EUA in the welfare of producers and about 2500 million EUA in that of consumers. Through increased contributions to the Community budget, the agreement is estimated to have cost taxpayers an extra 2200 million EUA. Adding together these three amounts, the overall effect of the 1980 price package is estimated at about 1900 million EUA, two-fifths of which is experienced by Germany. Ireland and Denmark are the main exceptions to the general pattern, although the amounts involved are small compared to the effects on the larger countries, while the effect of the package on the Netherlands is almost neutral.

The effects of harmonising prices to the common production-weighted average price within the Community depend on the pattern of 'green' exchange rates and monetary compensatory amounts (MCAs) which such a move would eliminate. In the circumstances of mid-1980, the overall effect, as shown in Section II of Table 10.1, is a net loss to producers and gain to consumers of 2100-2200 million EUA. A taxpayer gain of 1200 million EUA results in a significant positive effect, of 1400 million EUA, mainly through adjustments in Germany and the United Kingdom. These results differ somewhat from earlier studies[6] of harmonisation proposals on account of the substantial alterations in exchange rates which took place during 1979 and 1980. However, one conclusion reached by earlier researchers is reinforced, namely that movement to truly common prices is likely to earn neither political nor economic endorsement, without regard to the level of those common prices relative to existing national levels.

Whilst the target of exact Community self-sufficiency has little to commend it from a theoretical point of view,[7] the effect of such a policy change, given the current surplus production in the Community, is at least of interest in terms of its potential effect on the budget. Self-sufficiency in products currently in surplus eliminates the disposal cost to the taxpayer, a cost which in 1980 amounted to a net 5600 million EUA. Such a policy would therefore go a long way to easing if not removing the current crisis in the EC. As shown in Section III of Table 10.1, this is achieved only at the considerable cost of nearly 10000 million EUA to producers. Consumers however would gain by 7200 million EUA if the policy objective were achieved by a cut in agricultural product prices, as is assumed here. If, however, the objective were to be pursued by producer co-responsibility levies (taxes) then consumers would be unaffected and, in essence, most of the gain shown here as accruing to consumers would, through the levy receipts, accrue to taxpayers instead. The loss suffered by producers would remain unchanged.[8] The overall benefit to the Community of eliminating surpluses is estimated at over 3000 million EUA.

The 'academic' policy option of a free market shows a net gain of 11000 million EUA to the EC as a whole and proportionately substantial gains to all countries except the three 'specialist' exporters, the Netherlands, Ireland and Denmark. These net gains are, of course, achieved at substantial expense to farmers. It is this fact which, above all others, is the most obvious reason why a policy change which would involve substantial reductions in the transfers generated by the CAP are not politically acceptable, despite the direct and obvious savings to taxpayers of some 11000 million EUA of scarce public funds. While these values are of theoretical interest, realistic discussion of policy change requires more restricted analysis.

POLICY CHANGES AND PRICE CHANGES

Within the Council of Ministers' discussions on the CAP the central theme is agricultural price changes. The major meeting of the Council, the annual price-fixing negotiations, is concerned with little else. Producers and consumers are, similarly, most directly influenced and affected by the CAP through the levels of price administered by the policy. It is to be expected, then, that price changes are of central political importance in the development of the CAP. Tables 10.2 and 10.3 show by country and by commodity the average price changes which underlie the estimates made in this study. In all cases the price changes shown are in real terms, having taken account of the differing rates of inflation in the member countries in the case of the 1980 price package and defined in real 1980 terms in the remaining cases.

The achievement of agreement in the Council of Ministers to an annual price package are highlighted by the real price changes implicit in the 1980 price agreement. Inflation rates disguise real effects, and hence distorts the political advantages and disadvantages of the package as announced. The package in fact is seen to have had a remarkably even effect across member states despite their very different production patterns and the widely different inflation rates which each experienced in 1980.

170

Table 10.2 : Average Price Changes Under Policy Alternatives, By Country.

Average price change for all CAP commodities resulting from a change in the CAP from the 1980 base position to the alternative specified.

Country	1980 Price Package	Price Harmonisation	Community Self-Sufficiency	Free Market
		(percentages)		
Germany	-4.3	-9.8	-13.5	-38.3
France	-4.3	0.0	-12.8	-28.3
Italy	-4.3	0.0	-9.4	-27.7
Netherlands	-4.1	-1.8	-14.7	-36.2
Belgium/Luxembourg	-4.7	-1.8	-14.8	-34.6
United Kingdom	-4.3	-3.3	-16.0	-30.4
Ireland	-3.9	1.3	-17.7	-30.3
Denmark	-4.4	0.0	-16.6	-34.3
EC 9	-4.3	-2.9	-13.5	-31.9

SOURCE : Authors' estimates.

NOTE : Average prices are weighted by production quantities and thus changes reflect different commodity price changes and different mixes of production in the member states. Detailed discussion of these estimates is contained in Chapter 6.

Table 10.3 : Average Price Changes Under Policy Alternatives, By Commodity

Commodity	1980 Price Package	Price Harmonisation	Community Self-Sufficiency	Free Market
		(percentages)		
Common Wheat	-4.5	-2.5	-26.7	-19.7
Barley	-4.5	-2.9	-30.6	-31.6
Maize	-4.5	-0.4	0.0	-29.2
Sugar	-5.3	-2.8	-20.4	-20.4
Pigmeat	-5.5	-3.7	-14.9	-49.3
Beef & Veal	-4.0	-2.7	0.0	-34.0
Butter	-2.3	-2.9	-27.3	-46.9
Skim Milk Powder	-4.9	-3.5	-75.2	-45.1

SOURCE : Authors' estimates.

NOTE : Detailed discussion of the policy alternatives is contained in Chapters 5 and 6.

In addition, while the wide scope of the CAP offers many opportunities for trade-offs and compromise within the policy decisions, and while divided interests over agricultural policy and its consequences within nation states reduce the political damage of any decision which runs counter to farming interests, the package represents a balance between a drastic no-agreement cut in real prices, and the maintenance of real price levels to producers.

Inspection of the real changes implicit in the often-acclaimed goal of Community self-sufficiency suggest that larger cuts will have to come within the realms of political feasibility. Moreover, the underlying growth in production in excess of consumption due to technological and structural change is not insignificant (approximately two per cent per annum for dairy products, for example). This growth is ignored in these estimates, yet continued real price reductions would be necessary year after year, on top of the significant real reduction shown in Table 10.2, to maintain self-sufficiency and prevent the re-emergence of surpluses. Finally, the price reductions implicit in a move to free markets are clearly too large to be contemplated within the current political and institutional structure of the Community.

GAINERS AND LOSERS

The price changes discussed above are likely to be politically important because of their visibility to the electorate. The political importance of policy changes as a whole, however, will also be related to the extent of welfare gains and losses in relation to the numbers of people involved.

Although the net welfare gains or losses shown in Table 10.1 indicate overall gains from price reductions because of the reduced level of consumer and taxpayer transfer to producers, this result certainly does not provide a good indicator of political acceptability. The figures in Tables 9.1 and 9.8 showing the gains and losses per head provide more readily appreciated measures of the perceived welfare effects. Such figures are more likely to accord with politicians' interests in policy changes than are the total gross and net transfers.

Seen from this perspective, the ambiguity of the costs and benefits of a policy change becomes obvious. Until the EC budgetary ceiling is reached, the Council of Agricultural Ministers of the Community has as its primary, if not sole, concern the interests of farmers and farm workers. The influence of

budgetary (taxpayer) or consumer interests is only
indirect, through instructions and recommendations
from national governments, and therefore muted.
Under these circumstances the attraction of any
policy change which significantly damages farming
interests, even at substantial offsetting gains to
the other two groups, must quickly evaporate.

In fact, the calculation of net total gains and
losses (as in Table 10.1) can only be done on the
assumption that one unit of account as a gain to
consumers or taxpayers is exactly equivalent to
(that is, can be exactly offset by) a one unit of
account loss to producers. Since the 'target groups'
are of such widely different sizes, of widely
different political cohesiveness and wield substantially different political influence, such equal
weights are very unlikely to reflect the political
weight attached to each group.

ADJUSTMENT AND EFFICIENCY

While the pressures for change in the CAP have grown
stronger through the late 1970s, and show every sign
of increasing during the 1980s, the development of
the policy to date suggests that any change will be
evolutionary rather than revolutionary. Throughout
its history, the CAP has been developed in reaction
to pressures from outside rather than as a result
of active policy design and analysis of alternatives
by some central decision-making body. Without a
radical change in the political and administrative
structure of the European Community, the 'machinery'
of policy-making will ensure that any future development continues to react to pressures, and that the
policy will continue to evolve in the directions
indicated by these pressures.[9]

For this reason it is both useful and interesting to consider the idea of incremental changes in
policy towards a longer run objective. As the principal instruments of the CAP are prices, the main
'internal' changes to CAP (as opposed to 'external'
reforms of it) involve particular patterns of price
change. Having characterised each alternative policy
as a given configuration of commodity price changes,
it is a simple matter to consider incremental moves
towards (or away from) each alternative policy.
This approach offers two benefits. First, it permits study of the effects on parties of interest of
partial moves in a desirable direction, e.g. 10 per
cent of the way towards a free market. Second, it
enables the calculation of costs per unit of desired
effects. Chapter 9 presents results of such

calculations of the average and marginal costs,
using four definitions of 'cost', three measures of
'effect', and for four types of policy move.

To illustrate the findings of this analysis, in
order to raise farm incomes through the price mechanism, it appears more 'efficient' in terms of extra
FEOGA expenditure and taxpayer contributions to increase prices uniformly across all CAP products
rather than to concentrate the increases on surplus
or highly-protected products. The FEOGA cost of
each 1 EUA rise in farm incomes through across-the-
board price increases is 0.76 EUA (Table 9.6),
giving a cost-effectiveness coefficient of 0.76,
while the equivalent figure for taxpayer cost is
0.91. Collectively, taxpayers and consumers give up
1.77 EUA for each marginal EUA transferred to producers in this way - or CAP 'efficiency' of 56 per
cent, as opposed to somewhat lower figures of 55 and
52 per cent if the other two patterns of price increases are adopted. Conversely, to gain maximum
fiscal benefit, price reductions for products in
surplus, promise greater gains than reductions proportional to market protection, for equivalent costs
in lost farm incomes. The marginal costs and benefits of achieving other CAP goals - measured by
price levels and self-supply indices - are estimated
at 450-600 million EUA in resource terms for each
one per cent change in these measures. Again, some
types of policy move within CAP are more efficient
in terms of certain costs than others. Further,
such calculations may be performed at country level
(Table 9.7) and for the effects of policy moves per
agricultural worker on farms of different sizes
(Table 9.8). The results emphasise how regions with
large or labour-intensive farm businesses (such as
the Netherlands) are vulnerable to reductions in the
support which the CAP at present gives such farms.

CONCLUDING REMARKS

The 1980s seem likely to see re-emerging the endemic
problems of the CAP. The Community has absorbed the
United Kingdom market but agricultural production
continues to be encouraged and surpluses are growing. As they do so, the budgetary cost of disposing
of them grows and this generates problems not only
of raising the necessary finance but also of the distribution, between member states, of the burdens and
benefits of the EC budget.[10] Meanwhile, as economic
growth slows, the pressures on farm incomes increase.
The lack of improvement in both absolute levels of
farm incomes, and the maldistribution of CAP-induced

income benefits between regions, and between the larger, richer farmers and their poorer, smaller partners, have become more noticeable, and more obviously at odds with the policy objectives.

While agricultural structures and income distributions relative to the rest of society differ widely within the Community, the degree of national flexibility within the CAP afforded by the MCA mechanism has by now been fully exploited in many cases (e.g. UK, France), and its future scope has been reduced by the relative monetary stability achieved through the European Monetary System. At the same time, Community agreement on appropriate farm price levels is made even more difficult by differing national conditions, especially inflation rates. Falling agricultural incomes pose a threat to the major objective of the CAP which cannot be countered within the existing policy by anything other than an ever-increasing level of price support and budgetary expenditure. Yet maintenance of market and budgetary balance can only be achieved, within the current CAP mechanisms, at the expense of farm incomes. The differences in political importance and weights attached to these conflicting objectives between member states makes agreement on policy direction increasingly difficult or expensive.

However, from time to time conditions can change to abate the pressures on a CAP. For example, in 1981, the relatively high levels of world prices and the significant contributions being made to Community financial resources through the positive MCA levies on imports in Germany and the United Kingdom temporarily eased the budgetary pressures. Furthermore, the 'prudent' price policy of the Community over the late 1970s, although cushioned by MCAs, have a delayed effect on the growth of agricultural production. Greater use of producer co-responsibility levies (advanced by the Commission as part of the 1981 farm price package)11 would encourage this trend towards less rapid growth in agricultural output, and also would provide additional Community revenue.12 As a result, the widely-heralded collapse of the CAP may yet be some way off. There is considerable scope for political and administrative ingenuity and compromise to delay the exhaustion of the Community budget. Policy changes evolving in this way will, of course, involve numerous problems between the member states. This is especially so if they are accompanied by declining levels of real farm incomes through direct levies on producers - the principle of co-responsibility. Provided these problems - in particular, the

shielding of smaller farms and poorer regions from
the full impact of such measures - can be kept within bounds, then producer co-responsibility for the
CAP may be accepted as preferable to the alternatives of an increase in VAT contributions, or a
wholesale reform of the CAP.

One proposal[13] to relieve the current budget
situation but to maintain pressure on members to reformulate the CAP is that of 'surplus contributions'
as an addition to current own resources. In
essence, the suggestion is that a new element be
added to the Community's own resources, based explicitly on the cost of disposing of agricultural
surpluses and bearing on each member state in the
proportion to total production of each commodity in
surplus accounted for by that member. This proposal
would remove the current budgetary problem as far as
the CAP is concerned and reflect to member states
the taxpayer costs of further developments of the
CAP, especially price changes. However, it leaves
the underlying problems of perverse distribution
between producers, consumers and taxpayers unaffected.

As the Community expands, increasing the
heterogeneity of political economic and agricultural
structures as well as of culture and language, the
difficulties of achieving consensus for reform will
grow. This might be supposed to reinforce the conclusion that change in agricultural policy will be
incremental rather than radical. However, enlargement might also work in the opposite direction,
precipitating more dramatic changes. Faced with
such a wide range of possibilities the professional
CAP analyst must try to provide for the public and
the policy-maker indications of the magnitude of the
costs and benefits of a variety of changes in the
policy. The specific changes chosen for analysis in
the present study may not in the event prove politically acceptable, but they serve to illustrate how
the conflicts of interest which inevitably accompany
change in an important and supra-national policy
area can be analysed and estimated in the case of
the CAP. It is in the longer-term interests of all
that economic analysis contributes to the solution
of the difficulties that lie ahead.

NOTES

1.   Commission of the European Communities: "Reflections on the Common Agricultural Policy" COM(80) 800
final, December 1980, p.3.

2.   See,for example, Chapter 2, Table 2.1.
3.   Although the country with the largest self-
sufficiency ratio (Ireland) also happens to be the
poorest country on a GNP per head basis, other
inter-country transfers are from poorer importing
countries (the United Kingdom and Italy) to relatively rich exporting countries (Netherlands, Belgium,
Luxembourg, Denmark and France).
4.   The gains and losses shown here are based on
estimates of the final or long-run effects of the
real price changes for each commodity on consumption
and production levels. In the latter case, particularly, one would not expect these effects to be
fully reflected in actual production levels for
three to five years and perhaps longer, that being
the time normally required for production practices
to adjust fully to price changes. On the other
hand, these gains and losses do not take account of
the continual underlying increase in production due
to technological and structural change, nor do they
take account of any (small) secular increase in consumption through time as populations and incomes
increase. The net 'welfare' effects depend also on
the assumption that the supply response curves reflect the true marginal social value of output.
5.   Direct CAP receipts and expenditure (import
levies and export refunds) are included in the producer and consumer effects, producers receiving the
benefit of export refunds and consumers paying (in
effect) the import levies. MCA taxes and subsidies
are similarly already included in the producer and
consumer effects. The VAT contribution rates used
here reflect the effects of the 1980 budgetary
settlement for the United Kingdom, by which the contribution rate is effectively reduced for the United
Kingdom and correspondingly increased for other
member states.
6.   See, for example, T. Heidhues, T.E. Josling,
C. Ritson and S. Tangermann, Common Prices and
Europe's Farm Policy, Trade Policy Research Centre,
Thames Essay, 1978, London.
7.   C. Ritson, Self Sufficiency and Food Security,
Centre for Agricultural Strategy Paper 8, 1980,
Reading explores the economic arguments and analysis
of self-sufficiency as a worthwhile agricultural
objective in and of itself in some detail. While
the argument is mainly directed at Britain, the conclusion that a primary goal of self-sufficiency has
no economic merit is more generally valid.
8.   The loss suffered by producers from a co-
responsibility levy designed to eliminate the difference between production and consumption levels could

be mitigated if, and only if, the levy were applied
on an individual producer basis and then only to
production in addition to the base 'quantum' for
each producer. The sum of all producer quantums
would in this case have to be set at the same level
as current EC consumption. In effect this system
would amount to the establishment of rigid individual
producer quotas which suffer from several serious
theoretical and practical drawbacks. See, for
example, Denis Bergmann (senior economist, INRA,
Paris), "Possible alternatives to the CAP and their
economic consequences", paper to the Agricultural
Economics Society Conference, The CAP in the 1980s,
2 December, 1980.
9. The history of the development of the CAP well
illustrates this evolutionary characteristic. See
Chapter 2 and associated references.
10. See Chapter 2 for details of the growth of CAP
and total expenditure compared with the growth in
the Community's own resources. The Commission's
"Reflections" (see Note 1 above) also discuss the
emerging problems of the CAP
11. Commission for the European Communities, Green
Europe Newsletter, "Common agricultural prices
1981/82, Commission's Proposals", February 1981,
Agricultural Information Service of the Directorate-
General for Agriculture, Brussels.
12. The effects of co-responsibility levies,
especially in comparison with price reductions, are
explored by the authors of this study in a paper to
the Agricultural Economics Society Conference.
Aberdeen, April 1981, "Some development options for
the Common Agricultural Policy", J. agric. Econ, 32
(3), September 1981.
13. This proposal is developed in more detail in
the paper referred to in the previous note.

INDEX